EMMAUS BIBLE RESOURCES

G000155005

A Rebellious Prophet

JONAH

EMMAUS BIBLE RESOURCES

A Rebellious Prophet

JONAH

JOY TETLEY

Church House Publishing
Church House
Great Smith Street
London SW1P 3NZ

ISBN 0 7151 4986 5

Published 2003 by Church House Publishing

Tel: 020 7898 1594
Fax: 020 7898 1449
Email: copyright@c-of-e.org.uk

Cover design by Church House Publishing
Typeset in Franklin Gothic and Sabon

Printed in England by The Cromwell Press Ltd,
Trowbridge, Wiltshire

Contents

How to use this book

The *Emmaus Bible Resources* can be used on your own, with a small group and with a whole church or group of churches (or any combination of the three).

On your own

Each chapter is divided into six parts ending with a short prayer or meditation.

You can use the studies as part of a daily time of Bible reading and prayer.

Or you can read the chapter with the biblical text at a single sitting.

A simple Order for Daily Prayer is provided at the back of the book.

With a small group

The group can be three friends, a husband and wife, an ongoing home group or one drawn together for these studies.

Each member of the group should read a chapter of this book and the biblical text between meetings.

At the end of each chapter, you will find a 'Guideline for groups'.

Each group will need a convenor to guide you through this material.

With the whole church

The material is designed so that a church or group of churches could use it as the basis of Sunday and midweek material for learning and discussion.

A group of Sundays can be identified as appropriate for a series of sermons on Jonah. Tables of readings and other resources are provided in the Liturgical Resources section at the end of the book.

Members of the congregation who wish to engage with the text for themselves can then be encouraged to read this book as a study guide alongside the sermon series. Those who wish to do so can also meet in small groups during the week.

Overview of Emmaus Bible Resources		
Individual usage	**Small group usage**	**Whole church usage**
The book can form the basis of a daily time of reading and prayer.	Each chapter can be used as a 90-minute study.	A short series of sermons is envisaged, one for each chapter.

Guidelines
- To help the group dynamics – so that they understand each other and the biblical text better;
- For discussion questions – in order to assist reflection and application;
- For practical 'follow-on' activities that arise from each study.

Liturgical Resources
This section suggests ways of incorporating the study material into the ministry of the word as the congregation gathers on Sundays or during the week.
There is also an order for Daily Prayer.

Introduction to *Emmaus Bible Resources*

The two disciples walk along the road to Emmaus with Jesus,
although they do not recognize him. As they walk together,
Jesus interprets and opens the Scriptures to them. They have no books or texts
with them but these disciples would already be familiar with many of the words
of Scripture and would perhaps have learned them by heart.

From the earliest times, Christians have read the Scriptures on their own, together
and in the company of the risen Christ. Every act of Christian worship has at its
centre the public reading of the Bible, the word of God. Through reading and
study of the Scriptures, our Christian faith is refreshed, strengthened, challenged
and renewed. As Paul writes to Timothy:

> All scripture is inspired by God and is useful for
> teaching, for reproof, for correction, and for training
> in righteousness, so that everyone who belongs to
> God may be proficient, equipped for every good work
> (2 Timothy 3.16-17).

It is becoming harder to live as a Christian. Every Christian needs to live out
the truth of their baptism: each one of us is called to Christian discipleship
and Christian service according to the gifts God has given to us.

The *Emmaus Bible Resources* are offered as a way of encouraging individuals,
small groups and congregations to engage with the text of Scripture in order
that they may be built up and grow in Christian life, faith and service.

As with *Emmaus: The Way of Faith*, we have tried to combine sound and
orthodox Christian theology with good educational practice on the one hand
and a commitment to equip the whole Church for mission on the other.

Each book in the series is complete in itself and is intended as a guide either to
a passage of Scripture or to a short series of passages grouped around a central
theme. We hope to publish two or three books in the series each year. Normally
the passage will be part of a longer book within the Bible, or it may be the whole
of one of the shorter books.

Each book in the series is largely written by one person (whose name appears on the cover) but has been edited by the original group of authors. We hope, over time, to involve others outside the original group in developing new material for the series.

Each author has been asked to write for a general Christian audience but to bring to the work insights from the Christian tradition of interpretation and the best of contemporary biblical scholarship. Notes and references have been kept to a minimum although there are some ideas for further reading. Each book also encourages a variety of learning styles in terms of individual study and reflection and group interaction.

Wherever possible, some of the material in each book has been piloted both with individuals and in small groups. We are very grateful to the churches, groups and individuals who have assisted in this way. The new series can be used just as well by individuals and churches who have not used the original *Emmaus* material as by those who have been using it for many years.

Five years after the publication of *Emmaus: The Way of Faith*, we are surprised and humbled at the many ways God has used the material, through the ministry and prayers of many Christian people and for the building up of Christians, of churches and, ultimately we pray, of the kingdom of God. Our prayer for this new series is that it may be used by God in similar ways and to the same ends.

Stephen Cottrell
Steven Croft
John Finney
Felicity Lawson
Robert Warren

Acknowledgements

This book was produced in the midst of the hectic schedule of an archdeacon's life and the author is therefore especially grateful to her husband for all his encouragement and support in the travail. The book is dedicated to him. Warm thanks are also due to Jean Armitage, my secretary, who valiantly typed up a good deal of material when the home computer crashed.

The publisher gratefully acknowledges permission to reproduce copyright material in this book. Every effort has been made to trace and contact copyright holders. If there are any inadvertent omissions, we apologize to those concerned and undertake to include suitable acknowledgements in all future editions.

Unless otherwise indicated, the prayers and reflections at the end of each section of text are by the author.

Bible quotations are from *The New Revised Standard Version of the Bible* copyright © 1989 by the Division of Christian Education of the National Council of Churches in the USA. All rights reserved.

Extracts from *Common Worship: Service and Prayers for the Church of England* (Church House Publishing, 2000), *Common Worship: Daily Prayer, Preliminary Edition* (Church House Publishing, 2002) and *New Patterns for Worship* (Church House Publishing, 2002) are copyright © The Archbishops' Council of the Church of England.

An Introduction to Jonah

The Book of Jonah is something of an eccentric among the prophetic literature in the Bible. Unlike the other prophetic books, it is not made up of a collection of oracles or 'words from the Lord'. Rather, it is a vivid story, a narrative drama, full of irony and humour, whilst carrying a challenging prophetic message. In this respect, though it is in a more extended form, it is not unlike the parables of Jesus. Like those parables, it is most certainly intended to be a story with a meaning – whether it is based on actual events, or composed as a telling tale.

Quite when this remarkable narrative came to be written is difficult to determine. Its language and attitudes seem to point to a date some time after the Babylonian Exile, that is, after the latter part of the fifth century BC. But, whatever its precise provenance, the message of the book is timeless. That message is primarily to do with the character of God, and the diverse nature of human response to God. It is also interesting to note that a significant sub-theme draws our attention to God's positive relationship with non-human creation.

Jonah

The central human character of the book is a fascinating figure. We might call him a tragicomic anti-hero. His name means 'dove'. The psalmist longed for the wings of a dove, that he might fly far away from the trouble that was assailing him (Psalm 55.4-8). Jonah 'the dove' actually took flight, but he soon discovered that he could not escape 'the raging wind and tempest' born of God's determined will. Running away from the presence of the Lord is not always the easy option it might seem.

We know very little about Jonah's identity and life-history. He is simply described in the narrative as 'son of Amittai'. A prophet of the same name and parentage is referred to in 2 Kings 14.25. This Jonah spoke the word of the Lord to King Jeroboam II of Israel (786–746 BC). It was an encouraging word, promising the restoration of Israel's borders and the deliverance of the nation from destruction by the enemy (at that time, Syria). But it was also during Jeroboam's reign that Amos and Hosea communicated God's hard words to a prosperous society that was losing its soul. The blessing of God is not to be taken as a permissive cover for complacency and corruption. For Jonah, son of Amittai, however, the protection and promotion of national interests seems to have been the priority.

It may well be that the Book of Jonah takes the eighth-century prophet as its starting point, possibly using traditional material about him. What emerges is a character from whom the people of God – and their spiritual leaders – can learn some vital, if uncomfortable, lessons. Jonah was not just a *reluctant* spokesman for God; he was also a disobedient one. He was prejudiced, petulant, resentful and sulky. He wanted God on his own terms. Though he was willing to rejoice in his own deliverance (see Jonah 2), he could not allow (let alone rejoice) that God might want to save those outside Jonah's boundaries of acceptability. Yet God chose Jonah to proclaim just such a saving opportunity to an alien, despised culture. And God persisted in his choice. God has his reasons; and God does not easily let go.

There are still many Jonahs. And God has not changed.

The shape of this book

Each chapter of this book works through a chapter of the Book of Jonah. Within each chapter there are six sections, ending with a prayer, designed to assist a pattern of daily study and reflection. These sections not only explore the text of Jonah, but also consider how Jonah relates to other themes and writings in the Scriptures. It is always helpful, and sometimes challenging, to see books of the Bible in the wider context of other scriptural material. It is also crucial to ask ourselves what the biblical texts have to say to us now, in our age and situation. The author hopes that these musings on Jonah will help in that task.

This book further contains guidelines for group study and some suggested liturgical resources for those congregations who would want to incorporate sustained reflection on Jonah into their church services.

However the book is used, may it somehow be a small window onto God's sovereign grace and love.

Chapter 1
A Prophet in Rebellion – Jonah 1

No way (1.1-3)

> Now the word of the Lord came to Jonah son of
> Amittai, saying, 'Go at once to Nineveh, that great
> city, and cry out against it; for their wickedness has
> come up before me.' But Jonah set out to flee to
> Tarshish from the presence of the Lord. He went down
> to Joppa and found a ship going to Tarshish; so he
> paid his fare and went on board, to go with them to
> Tarshish, away from the presence of the Lord.

The story starts abruptly with a directive word from the Lord: 'Go at once to
Nineveh.' There is no setting of the scene. Attention is immediately propelled to
the command of God. Here is a God who speaks – and expects an immediate
and obedient response. Here is a God who is aware of (and distressed by) human
wickedness – even when it is perpetrated by those who do not belong to the
community with whom God has made covenant. Here is a God who takes bold
initiatives to open the eyes of sinners (whatever their pedigree), that they might
see the truth of their condition – and, in repenting, turn and receive the grace of
divine forgiveness. And here is a God who chooses to use human agents to express
his concern and longing to save – thus opening himself, as in this case, to the perils
of a less than ideal cooperator.

When we read the Scriptures, when we look at the pilgrimage of God's people
through the ages, when we reflect on our own experience, it quickly strikes us
that, again and again, God calls and uses those who are far from perfect. Many of
the biblical 'big names' had, to say the least, significant character flaws. Think of
Jacob, for example. The way he treats his brother, Esau, is hardly a model for
good family relationships. He takes advantage of his brother's weakness to rob
him of his birthright (Genesis 25.29-34). In collusion with his mother, he later
deprives Esau of his father's blessing by trickery and deception (Genesis 27).
Despite this, Jacob becomes a key figure in God's purposes. The name given him
by God (Israel) becomes synonymous with God's people. Other examples of God's
surprising choices are as numerous as the sand on the seashore!

Time would certainly fail to tell of them all, but we might do well to recall especially the ones Jesus chose to be his twelve disciples and mission partners. They were, without doubt, a motley crew. They had few obvious 'qualifications' to be spiritual leaders. Indeed, they often tried Jesus' patience by their failure to understand his teaching (Mark 4.13; 7.17; 8.17-21; 8.32-33; 9.32). Along the way, they seem to have been frequently preoccupied with arguing as to who among them was the greatest (Mark 9.33-35; 10.35-44). When the great crisis came, one of them betrayed Jesus, one denied him, and all of them ran away (Mark 14.43-46, 50, 66-72). Strange choices, from a human point of view. Yet God sees beyond their shortcomings to their deeper potential.

The reluctance of those chosen is also a constantly recurring theme. Even the great Moses took some persuading (see Exodus 3 and 4). Initially, when Moses encounters the holiness of God by means of a burning bush, he is awestruck (Exodus 3.1-4). Yet, when the Lord begins to set out how Moses is to be his key agent in delivering his people from Egypt, devotion quickly gives way to argument. Though Moses is 'afraid to look at God', his fear of what God is asking him to do rapidly eclipses his fear of the divine presence. Though he insists to God that he is 'slow of speech and slow of tongue' (Exodus 4.10), he soon finds a voice to object. And, after a lengthy tussle with God, Moses desperately utters a prayer with which many will have identified over the centuries: 'O my Lord, please send someone else' (Exodus 4.13). Though certain concessions are made, the Lord does not oblige!

We see from the behaviour of both Moses and the Twelve that, at critical moments in the story of salvation, God's plans are jeopardized by human weakness and obduracy. Jonah (who does not even bother to argue) is in good company. And he, too, discovers that, despite many a setback, God perseveres.

All this should bring home to us that God can weave the less than perfect into his creative working. God can use human shortcomings as material for constructive ministry. With this God, all things and all situations have the potential to open up opportunities for the exercise of grace. That should give us hope indeed.

Jonah's intended destination (at least from God's point of view) is Nineveh (located in the north of modern Iraq), sometime capital city of Assyria, an aggressive foreign power that frequently threatened the security of the peoples of Israel and Judah, particularly in the eighth and seventh centuries BC. Assyria conquered the northern kingdom of Israel, taking its capital, Samaria, in 721 BC. Going to Nineveh would be no holiday. It was not an expedition Jonah was prepared to undertake. Distant Tarshish (probably in southern Spain) seemed rather more attractive, even though it meant travelling a very long way from home. Surely God would not pursue him to a far country. God would find someone else for the unpalatable mission to Nineveh. No way could God's presence extend as far as Tarshish. God's presence belonged, after all, in the midst of God's holy people.

But Jonah was to learn that saying 'no way' to God is by no means the end of the matter. God will not take 'no' for an answer. And Jonah was also to learn that God, too, is itinerant – and that God could be a disturbing travelling companion. God's 'presence' is not limited to any geographical location, to any 'holy' place or community. God is there at all times and in all places. So the writer of Psalm 139 discerned, using words that are very pertinent for Jonah – and for all of us:

> Where can I go from your spirit?
> Or where can I flee from your presence?
>
> (Psalm 139.7; see also vv. 8-12).

Nowhere. That's the answer. Not even Tarshish. Even though, in human terms, Jonah was a legitimate passenger (he had paid his fare!), God had booked him on a different route.

The reason Jonah fled is not spelt out at this point in the narrative. It comes to light towards the end (4.1-3). We shall consider it further in that context. Meanwhile, the writer of the story leaves us with an unspoken and open question: why, exactly, does Jonah disobey God?

Mysterious God,
you know us through and through.
We long for a sense of your presence,
and yet are startled by your word.
Who are we, that we can do your bidding?
Why do you ask so hard a thing of us?
Your way, not mine, we sing;
but this? Your way, perhaps. Not ours – yet.

Give us grace, God, both to know and to do your will.

Storm at sea (1.4-6)

> But the Lord hurled a great wind upon the sea, and
> such a mighty storm came upon the sea that the ship
> threatened to break up. Then the mariners were afraid,
> and each cried to his god. They threw the cargo that
> was in the ship into the sea, to lighten it for them.
> Jonah, meanwhile, had gone down into the hold of the
> ship and had lain down, and was fast asleep. The
> captain came and said to him, 'What are you doing,
> sound asleep? Get up, call on your god! Perhaps the
> god will spare us a thought so that we do not perish.'

The consequences of Jonah's disobedience are dramatic. A mighty storm
breaks, endangering both the ship on which he is travelling and the lives of its
crew. Amongst the sailors, fear and panic work their work. Desperate measures
have to be taken. And, in the midst of it all, Jonah goes down into the hold and
falls asleep.

First, Jonah runs away from God's calling. Others can do what he has no
stomach for. Then Jonah hides away from the storm. Others can cope with
the calamity his behaviour has brought about.

Jonah is no hero. Quite the reverse. But God will not allow him the luxury of
his cowardice – nor, indeed, of his refusal to cooperate. Jonah is aroused from
sleep to play his part in dealing with the crisis. He must pray. It is ironic and
instructive that it is those from outside his own believing community who call
on Jonah to get going at last with what should have been his first response.
Frightened sailors, who have no knowledge of Jonah's God, point up the prime
and urgent need for prayer.

In times of great turbulence, many people still turn instinctively to prayer, whether
or not they overtly practise a faith. On Jonah's boat 'each cried to his god'. In the
storms of life that cry ever goes up. It is uttered in desperation and helplessness,
often in a very raw manner. It is prayer 'out of the deep' (see Psalm 130.1), from
the honesty of where people really are. Frequently, it is a desperate, last resort
(and most certainly none the worse for that). Throughout the Scriptures there
are many examples of such cries for help. The Psalms are full of them (see, for
example, Psalms 7.1; 10.1; 13.1).

Often, in calling out to God, the psalmists use imagery to do with storm, tempest and flood. Such imagery is very telling. Even now, with all our scientific knowledge and technology, the sheer power of the natural forces around us can be fearful and overwhelming. When the full power of nature is unleashed, whether in actual fact or as a metaphor to describe human experience, it can help us to express our terror, confusion and helplessness.

> Save me, O God,
>> for the waters have come up to my neck.
> I sink in deep mire,
>> where there is no foothold;
> I have come into deep waters,
>> and the flood sweeps over me.
>
> (Psalm 69.1-2)

We don't need a great deal of imagination to identify with that heart-cry. The language is frighteningly graphic. So is that of the poet who produced Psalm 107. In the course of that psalm, we come across this description of storm at sea:

> Some went down to the sea in ships,
>> doing business on the mighty waters;
> they saw the deeds of the Lord,
>> his wondrous works in the deep.
> For he commanded and raised the stormy wind,
>> which lifted up the waves of the sea.
> They mounted up to heaven, they went down
>> to the depths;
>> their courage melted away in their calamity;
> they reeled and staggered like drunkards,
>> and were at their wits' end.
> Then they cried to the Lord in their trouble,
>> and he brought them out from their distress;
> he made the storm be still,
>> and the waves of the sea were hushed.
> Then they were glad because they had quiet,
>> and he brought them to their desired haven.
> Let them thank the Lord for his steadfast love,
>> for his wonderful works to humankind.
>
> (Psalm 107.23-31)

We can see and feel the scene. Like Jonah's sailing companions, and many others down the ages who have found themselves in peril on the seas, the people depicted by the psalmist were 'at their wits' end'. It is interesting to notice that, according to the psalmist, this is the Lord's doing. It was God who 'commanded and raised the stormy wind, which lifted up the waves of the sea'. So it is also in the Jonah narrative. It was the Lord who 'hurled a great wind upon the sea' (1.4). This clearly raises questions about the nature and behaviour of God. If events that create such chaos are really 'acts of God', what are we to make of this God?

Throughout the Scriptures, God's sovereignty over the elements recurs as a strong theme. It is there at the outset in the creation narrative of Genesis 1. It is there when God all but destroys wayward creation by bringing 'a flood of water on the earth' (Genesis 6 – 8). That story ends with a promise:

> As long as the earth endures,
>> seedtime and harvest, cold and heat,
> summer and winter, day and night,
>> shall not cease.

(Genesis 8.22)

Here is a very important indicator. The God of the Bible is quite clearly in control. But divine control is not exercised in a random or malicious manner. God's power is used to counter the forces of evil, chaos, destruction and sin. The purpose is salvation – the fulfilment of creation's potential for good, the working out of wholesome blessing.

That truth becomes clear and becomes flesh in Jesus. In Jesus we encounter 'the power of God and the wisdom of God' (1 Corinthians 1.24). Looking to Jesus points us to the heart of what God's power is like and what it is used for. It is not what we expect. It is expressed to its full extent on the cross – on what, in human terms, is perceived as utter powerlessness. Yet it is the power of sheer love taking on all the forces of negativity that the world can muster.

On the way to Calvary, Jesus, for love's sake, does many 'acts of power'. One is particularly worthy of reflection in the light of the opening chapter of Jonah. It is the occasion when a bad storm blows up on the Sea of Galilee. Jesus and his disciples are caught up in the tempest as they are crossing over to the other side of the lake. The disciples are terrified, feeling in their panic that their end has come. But Jesus – like Jonah, but for different reasons – is asleep in the stern of the boat. When the disciples cry out to him to save them, he gets up and rebukes the wind, and says to the sea, 'Peace! Be still!' Then, Mark tells us, 'the wind ceased, and there was a dead calm' (Mark 4.35-41). Jesus, the Son of God, is lord of the storm and saviour of those in need. And, unlike Jonah, he acts appropriately.

To these matters we shall return.

'Lord, teach us to pray,'
your disciples asked.
And now, in spite of ourselves,
we are bidden to pray.
Our backsliding has come back with a vengeance.
How can we pray in this strange turmoil,
at the bidding of those who know you not?
Perhaps they know you better than we do.

Lord, teach us to pray.

Searching questions (1.7-10)

The sailors said to one another, 'Come, let us cast lots, so that we may know on whose account this calamity has come upon us.' So they cast lots, and the lot fell on Jonah. Then they said to him, 'Tell us why this calamity has come upon us. What is your occupation? Where do you come from? What is your country? And of what people are you?' 'I am a Hebrew,' he replied. 'I worship the Lord, the God of heaven, who made the sea and the dry land.' Then the men were even more afraid, and said to him, 'What is this that you have done!' For the men knew that he was fleeing from the presence of the Lord, because he had told them so.

It is the terrified sailors who look beyond the natural for the significance of their predicament. Jonah is pinpointed as the focus of the disturbance and he is interrogated as to the reason. Their insistent, quick-fire questioning draws from him both a confession of faith and a confession of sin. Together, these confessions strike further terror into the hearts of his inquisitors. These sailors seem rather more aware of the enormity of his sin than does Jonah himself.

They also take the power of God more seriously, quickly making the connection between Jonah's sovereign creator God and the wildness of the elements around them. Jonah, on the other hand, though professing worship of a deity who is lord of all, thinks he can escape this God's presence, and, even in a crisis, needs prompting to pray. The implications of his creed appear to have escaped him.

We see the same pattern much later, in the responses to Jesus. So often, we learn from the Gospels, it is those on the edge and those outside who perceive and proclaim the truth of God. By contrast, again and again the chosen disciples fail to understand; and in the end they run away. According to Mark's Gospel, it is left to a Gentile centurion (and one involved in putting Jesus to death) to recognize and highlight the heart of the matter: 'Truly this man was God's Son!' (Mark 15.39). His insight penetrates the darkness of Calvary. From his perspective as part of the execution squad, he sees what the scattered disciples fail to see. He sees through human appearances and expectations to a far deeper truth. It is left to him (not the followers of Jesus) to discern in the manner of this man's dying the very presence of God.

The clear-sightedness of the outsider should never be underestimated, nor disallowed as somehow invalid. If God really is Lord of all, then divine communication will not be confined to what might be thought acceptable channels. What matters to God is to get the message through. Jonah needed to learn that, and so do all believers. The journey of belief is a challenging one. Getting to know God is risky as well as comforting. In love, and as we can bear it, God will ask much of us – not least asking us to see beyond our own horizons and secure frameworks. God meets us where we are but will not be domesticated on our terms. We cannot keep God as a pet or a crutch. 'The Lord, the God of heaven, who made the sea and the dry land' wants partners in the great enterprise of bringing salvation to the ends of the earth.

Whatever that means for us, if we try to run away we shall be both in good company and on to a loser. As Jonah found, God does not easily give up the pursuit. Over the centuries, many others have found the same. In biblical terms, we could reflect, for example, on those who tried to flee from God's presence because of a guilty conscience (so Adam and Eve in Genesis 1), because of depression and fear (so Elijah in 1 Kings 19 and the psalmist in Psalm 55.4-8) and because they did not want to do God's bidding (so, as we have seen, Moses' initial reluctance in Exodus 3 – 4).

Their attempts were to no avail. The One whom Francis Thompson called 'the hound of heaven'[1] sooner or later brings the flight to an end. Believing in God means accepting a God who may well do what we don't want as well as what we do. Yet in the end, saying 'yes', however reluctantly, opens us in some significant way to the heart of God. Whether we like it or not, God is a persistent and pervasive lover, whose love embraces the whole world.

If God can point up truth through outsiders, his methods can also be challenging. Throughout the Scriptures, again and again we find that the truth of the matter is brought into the open through searching questions. The process is very much a two-way one: God addresses questions to humankind but humankind also interrogates God. From beginning to end, the biblical texts spark and crackle with questions. A great variety of situations gives rise to them, from natural curiosity to matters of life and death. In engaging with Scripture, it is always important to be alert to its questions. Very often they impinge on our own life and pilgrimage.

In many ways, we have an interrogative God: a God who asks; a God who, out of steadfast love for us, asks for a response of love and commitment; a God who, for our deepest welfare, asks questions that search our hearts; a God who asks us to share his standards and his mission. And we are made in the image of this asking God. Our questions, it seems, are welcome at the throne of grace. Though we cannot presume to penetrate or control God's essential mystery and prerogatives (see, for example, Isaiah 40.12-31), we can, nonetheless, batter at heaven's door with that which disturbs and troubles us. The Psalms are full of such questioning, born out of desperate circumstances (see, for example, Psalms 22.1; 88.14; 89.46,49).

Psalm 22.1 reminds us that Jesus himself took advantage of the psalmist's words to carry his own questioning prayer in the awful bleakness of his dying ('my God, my God, why have you forsaken me?'). The example of Jesus matters above all. As well as sharing fully in our human experience, Jesus is the true revelation of God's character. When we look to Jesus, we see how God intended human beings to be. We also see right into the heart of God. If Jesus can ask such questions, then so can we – and so can God.

Throughout his earthly ministry, Jesus so often taught and furthered God's kingdom by facing people with questions. All the Gospel writings bear witness to this. His questions were invariably sharply direct and to the point: 'What do you think?' 'Who do you say that I am?' 'Do you believe this?' Such questions have not lost their relevance. Like the original hearers, we are left with the freedom to respond (or not) as we will.

As God poses questions through Jesus, so has God always questioned his people, either directly or through human agents. Of the latter, the prophets are a particular case in point. But here, in Jonah, we have a telling twist to that theme. It is God's prophet, Jonah, who is challenged with questions – and from those considered to be outside the boundaries of God's people. One of their most significant questions comes in verse 10: 'What is this that you have done?' This echoes God's question to Eve in the Garden of Eden (Genesis 3.13). The disobedience of Adam and Eve caused major disturbance in the relationship between humanity and God, humanity and creation. Jonah's disobedience, also, brings elemental disturbance in its wake. This time, God's question is uttered through 'pagan' sailors. It is they – rather than the insider called to be a prophet – who become the mouthpiece of God.

As we shall see, the book of Jonah itself ends with a question. On this occasion it comes directly from God. As so often with the parables of Jesus, we, as well as Jonah, are left to make of that what we will.

What have you done, my people?
We thought that was a question for others.
For Adam, perhaps;
for those who despised and rejected your servant,
wounded for our transgressions.
What have we done to deserve your rebuke?
Why do we hide from your way and your truth?
What do we fear?

Searching God, draw us back to yourself.

A lesson in faith (1.11-14)

Then they said to him, 'What shall we do to you, that the sea may quiet down for us?' For the sea was growing more and more tempestuous. He said to them, 'Pick me up and throw me into the sea; then the sea will quiet down for you; for I know it is because of

me that this great storm has come upon you.'
Nevertheless the men rowed hard to bring the ship
back to land, but they could not, for the sea grew
more and more stormy against them. Then they cried
out to the Lord, 'Please, O Lord, we pray, do not let us
perish on account of this man's life. Do not make us
guilty of innocent blood; for you, O Lord, have done
as it pleased you.'

The truth drawn out of him, Jonah now accepts that he must bear responsibility
for the storm stirred up by God. He must be given over to the divine tempest.
Others must not suffer further because of his guilt. Yet, even at this point, he
implicates others. Rather than hurling himself into the sea, he tells the sailors to
do the deed. True to form, Jonah adds to their distress and fear by loading on to
them a conscientious struggle with guilt. At this time of extremity, they could well
do without such critical decision-making. How good this prophet is at sucking
others into the maelstrom of his own disturbance.

Again, however, the response of the sailors sets a telling example. Despite the great
danger they are in, they will not lightly sacrifice Jonah's life. So, first, they attempt
an alternative strategy. They expend hard physical effort to row the ship back to
land, straining to save Jonah as well as themselves. When that proves to be of no
avail, they turn to prayer. It is, again, raw, honest prayer – a desperate crying out
to the Lord. They remind God that he has effectively put them in this parlous
situation and, therefore, surely cannot hold them guilty.

The biblical material presents us with a good many examples of those who not
only plead with God but who do so by arguing on the basis that God should
remember who he is and how he should behave. 'You, O Lord, have done as it
pleased you', the sailors point out to God. So don't blame us. The psalmists, too,
determinedly seek to prompt God's memory, as they call out for help.

> Have regard for your covenant . . .
> Rise up, O God, plead your cause;
>   remember how the impious scoff
>   at you all day long.

(Psalm 74.20,22)

In other words, '*Do* something, Lord. You have a covenant responsibility to your people. Don't let your enemies get away with it.' The ending of Psalm 89 (see vv. 34-52) has a similar approach, in a critical situation.

Deeply ingrained in the biblical perception of God is the conviction that (sometimes despite appearances) God will act with the integrity, fairness and justice that are integral to the divine nature. For such righteousness, it is worth taking the risk of struggling with God in prayer. So the psalmists believed. So also did the great patriarch, Abraham, who stubbornly persisted in challenging God about the fate of any righteous people who might be left in Sodom and Gomorrah (Genesis 18.22-33). God has taken Abraham into his confidence about the imminent fate of these depraved cities. Abraham's response is a confident (yet cannily diplomatic) intercession for those good folk, however small their number, who might still be in the cities. 'Will you indeed sweep away the righteous with the wicked?' asks Abraham of God, clearly expecting that God can only answer 'no'. The patriarch reinforces his expectation by daring to remind God of what should be divine behaviour: 'Far be it from you to do such a thing, to slay the righteous with the wicked, so that the righteous fare as the wicked! Far be that from you! Shall not the Judge of all the earth do what is just?' (v. 25).

How can the God of justice be less just than mere dust and ashes?

Other biblical characters worth exploring in this regard are Amos (see especially 7.1-9), Jeremiah (see especially 18.19-23; 20.7-13) and Job (see, for example, 13.13-22). In the scriptural record, holding to the righteousness of God and crying out for vindication and justice in the face of experience that seems to deny them are essential components in the vocation of God's people. Again and again, suffering and crisis are occasions for prayer and protest, rather than silent resignation.

The parable of Jesus contained in Luke 18.1-8 underlines the vital importance of persistence in prayer for the righteous action of God. Jesus 'told them a parable about their need to pray always and not to lose heart'. The story was about a widow who refused to give up demanding justice of a reluctant judge. The lesson to be drawn about God is by way of contrast: 'Listen to what the unjust judge says. And will not God grant justice to his chosen ones who cry to him day and night? Will he delay long in helping them? I tell you, he will quickly grant justice to them' (Luke 18.6-8).

The sailors in Jonah's story, 'outsiders' though they be in terms of the chosen community of faith, are keenly aware of the principles of justice. And they expect Jonah's God to act according to those principles. As Paul put it much later, in his letter to the Romans, they are like those Gentiles who 'show that what the law requires is written on their hearts' (Romans 2.15). Their faith and integrity are honoured. But first they have to take the enormous risk of consigning Jonah to what seems like certain death. If people and boat are to be saved, then this one must be sacrificed. Despite their best efforts and their reluctance, there seems no other way. By their faith, they are to become agents of salvation.

You, Lord, are supreme over all.
You do as you please.
Yet, Lord, God of mercy and justice,
hear the prayer of those who call on your name.
Remember for good those you have made,
and uphold those who stand against evil.

Lord, increase our faith.

Strange deliverance (1.15-17)

So they picked Jonah up and threw him into the sea;
and the sea ceased from its raging. Then the men
feared the Lord even more, and they offered a sacrifice
to the Lord and made vows.

But the Lord provided a large fish to swallow up
Jonah; and Jonah was in the belly of the fish three
days and three nights.

The sailors finally bring themselves to do the deed. As Jonah has told them to, they pick him up and throw him into the raging sea. By this decidedly physical action, they offer Jonah to the God of the storm. Jonah becomes, quite literally, the substance of their prayer.

As we noted earlier, the name 'Jonah' means 'dove'. Already, he has taken flight. The psalmist longed for the wings of a dove, so that he could fly away out of his troubles (Psalm 55.4-8). In this respect, Jonah has lived up to his name.

Metaphorically, he has used his wings to flee the unpalatable demands of God. Now God has (so to speak) caught up with him and Jonah has to fulfil another function of the dove in the culture of his time – that of a sin-offering. Doves were the poor person's offering, given instead of a more expensive animal, usually a lamb. The sacrifice of doves was intended to make atonement for various kinds of sin (see Leviticus 5.1,4,5; 12.6; 14.22; 15.29).

It is important for a later age and a different culture to try to grasp what lay behind a sacrificial system such as that detailed in Leviticus. One vital dimension was a keen sense of the absolute holiness of God. God was not someone to be trifled with. He was the God of storm and tempest, as well as the God of fair weather. Yet there was also the conviction that God had made gracious provision to enable less than holy human beings to live in a positive relationship with him. Sacrifices were believed to be a key ingredient in this provision. God desired communion with his human creation, wayward though it had proved to be. And God's desire could not but issue in action. That which offended God needed to be addressed but God had by no means turned his back on sinners. As Jonah was to discover, that included both foreign 'enemies' and rebellious prophets.

Sacrifices of animals (or produce) represented the self-offering of the giver in repentance or thanksgiving. That which was without blemish was offered to the holy God on behalf of those whose lack of holiness was all too apparent. In Jonah's case, when he finally accepts full responsibility for his sin and its consequences, he insists that he himself become the offering. In this circumstance, he perceives, no substitute will do. Jonah must again live up to his name, this time by taking upon himself the role of sacrificial 'dove'. He must be his own sin-offering. He has failed, when bidden to act as God's witness in Nineveh. In his disobedience, he has sought to turn his back on God. By doing so, he has put the lives of others in jeopardy. It has taken long enough – and the pressure of pagan sailors – for him to face up to his sin. Such determined and deliberate rebellion could only be atoned for by the handing over to God of his own life.

Such a perception of what God requires does at least underline the seriousness of what the Bible often calls 'high-handed' sin (see, for example, Isaiah 2.11-17; Jeremiah 44.22-23) – a deliberate flouting of God's commandments so as to cause offence to God and disturbance and suffering to other individuals and the wider community. Serious sin has serious consequences. That is not a popular notion in modern, western society, where the concept of 'sin' is so often dismissed as an unhealthy aberration, or treated as a joke. Yet human behaviour continues to issue

in atrocities, both small- and large-scale. In deriding the idea, we have not
lost the reality.

That said, it is important to remember that (as the old prayer puts it) God
'desireth not the death of a sinner but rather that he might turn from his
wickedness and live'.[2] The story of Jonah, in fact, proclaims that truth. The
story of Jesus (which, as we shall see, has not a few connecting themes with
Jonah) fleshes it out. We see from both Jonah *and* Jesus that God's way is not
destructive retribution but costly redemption. The meaning of sacrifice lies not,
after all, in a ritual system but at the heart of God.

In facing up to the storm, Jonah not only brings relief to the imperilled mariners.
He also – and unexpectedly – finds his own salvation. He does not meet his death.
He is swallowed up into the security of a large fish. What kind of fish is not
specified. There is no mention of a whale! The significance of the fish lies not in
its species but in the fact that God has brought it to the rescue. Like the natural
elements in their wildness, this creature is doing God's bidding and is an agent of
God's providence. The questions we should ask about this aspect of the story are
not zoological but theological. The message is that God is in control. This monster
of the deep holds no terror for God. It is a partner in ministry.

It is worth remembering that, in the mythology of the ancient Near East (Israel
included), sea monsters were fearsome beings who represented the deadly forces
of chaos. They featured strongly in the creation narratives of people in this region.
In Israel's scriptural tradition, though the role of the monster has been all but
written out of the creation narratives of Genesis 1 and 2, it does still surface from
time to time, usually under the name of Leviathan or Rahab (see Psalm 74.12-14;
Isaiah 27.1; 51.9).

Always the assertion is that God has triumphed over monstrous chaos. This
conviction connects with another and yet more telling perception: that if God
'made the sea and the dry land' (Jonah 1.9), then they and all that is in them are
under God's creative direction – even great creatures of the sea. Indeed, they are
not to be regarded as chaotic enemies but as God's friends, in whom God delights
(Psalm 104.24-26).

The particular version of 'Leviathan' that swallowed up Jonah was certainly
acting as the Lord's servant. So were the human seafarers who reluctantly threw
Jonah overboard into the stormy waters. In effect, and in strange circumstances,

those who have not known Jonah's God fulfil a priestly role. They make a fearful offering to God, the offering of a human life. In so doing they become agents of God's salvation in ways that go beyond their awareness or understanding. They even foreshadow the actions of God himself in Christ. But they do not see the full consequences of their act of faith. Those consequences reach far and wide (quite literally in the case of Nineveh). They thought they had consigned a man to death. What they do not see (in either sense) is that God's purpose is not death but life – both for Jonah and for those sinners to whom he finally goes with God's message.

Nonetheless, they experience for themselves a deliverance from disaster. The sea ceases its raging. Their reaction, true to form, is exemplary. They 'fear' even more the Lord they have encountered in crisis. 'Fear' in this context has the sense it frequently carries in the Scriptures – awe, respect and reverence in the presence of the divine. Such fear is not morbid but healthy. These sailors have not a little to teach us.

In a spirit of respectful thanksgiving, they now offer a more standard sacrifice to the Lord. They also make vows. Their desperate struggle has opened their eyes to the reality of God. For them, that demands a response of commitment, willingly given. Jonah, it seems, has been a missionary in spite of himself.

God's unheroic emissary stays 'in the belly of the fish three days and three nights'. That detail is reflected on by Jesus, as recorded in Matthew 12.38-41. We shall ponder later the significance of that passage. In its own setting in the Jonah story, the phrase stresses that Jonah was safely confined in this way for a full three days. Having lived with the Jonah narrative thus far, we can be sure that this state of affairs is integral to God's purpose. In this story, God is directing every detail. It may well be that the period of time specified is meant to connect in the reader's/hearer's mind with the period of time it was generally felt to be needed for a soul to journey to Sheol (there is a hint of this from Martha, the sister of Lazarus, at John 11.39). In Jonah's case, the journey that should have taken him to the underworld, to the land of shadows, in fact delivers him back to the land of the living. God has not finished with him yet.

You, Lord, have made all things
and uphold all things.
Remember for good all who seek to do right
and make offering in your name.
And, as you triumph over chaos
and turn death into new life,

let their vows and their lives
be honoured and acceptable in your sight.

God of salvation, we give you thanks and praise.

God's way – an overview of Jonah 1

The opening section of Jonah quickly engages our attention and stimulates our questioning. Why, exactly, is Jonah trying to run away from God? Why is he such a reluctant prophet and pray-er? What *is* going on in the midst of all this turmoil? What is set before us is tantalizing, to say the least. The narrator is clearly very skilled in making us intrigued, amused and perhaps not a little troubled. No space is wasted in doing so. Jonah's flight and the storm are briskly yet graphically portrayed. The characterization of prophet and mariners, though sparse, is correspondingly vivid and to the point. By the end of the episode, we feel that we know them in a significant way. We are also aware that they bring challenge and disturbance.

Already, in this first act of Jonah's drama, we are being faced with some of the fundamental concerns of the narrator. One is certainly to stress the sovereignty of God the Creator. Not even wind, storm and the might of the sea – traditional bearers of chaos and terror – can overwhelm God. God created them. They do God's bidding. The God who can 'hurl a great wind upon the sea' is one of supreme strength.

The author of 'Jonah' is by no means the only scriptural writer to emphasize the sovereignty of God over the natural world. The psalmists, particularly, convey this perception powerfully through their poetry:

> By awesome deeds you answer us with deliverance,
>   O God of our salvation;
> you are the hope of all the ends of the earth
>   and of the farthest seas.
> By your strength you established the mountains;
>   you are girded with might.
> You silence the roaring of the seas,
>   the roaring of their waves,
>   the tumult of the peoples.

> Those who live at earth's farthest bounds
>   are awed by your signs;
> you make the gateways of the morning
>   and the evening shout for joy.
>
> (Psalm 65.5-8)

> The heavens are yours, the earth also is yours;
> the world and all that is in it – you have founded them.
>
> (Psalm 89.11)

> The Lord is king, he is robed in majesty;
>   the Lord is robed, he is girded with strength.

> The floods have lifted up, O Lord,
>   the floods have lifted up their voice;
>   the floods lift up their roaring.
> More majestic than the thunders of mighty waters,
>   more majestic than the waves of the sea,
>   majestic on high is the Lord!
>
> (Psalm 93.1,3-4)

God is also frequently associated with natural phenomena in the exercise of his relations with humankind. A formative example of this surrounds God's presence on Mount Sinai, as he enters into covenant with the people he has delivered from Egypt.

> On the morning of the third day there was thunder and
> lightning, as well as a thick cloud on the mountain . . .
> Now Mount Sinai was wrapped in smoke, because the
> Lord had descended upon it in fire; the smoke went up
> like the smoke of a kiln, while the whole mountain
> shook violently. (Exodus 19.16,18)

In this critical case, the God of the storm comes not to destroy (he indicates how harm can be avoided, see Exodus 19.10-14), but to seal a committed relationship. In the case of Jonah, the God of the storm comes to rescue his prophet and his plan; there is a positive purpose. God's 'power and might' are not about tyrannical domination. They are not employed to bring about subservience through terror. God's dominion is exercised to work things together for good (see Romans 8.28), to draw out creative potential even in what seems negative and hopeless, to encourage that which leads to true well-being and peace.

Only searching faith can hold on to this conviction. In the opening section of the Book of Jonah, the pagan mariners show the way on this. They turn to prayer, they ask pertinent, penetrating questions, they act in faith even when they do not fully understand. Yet these folk are not only 'outsiders' in terms of the covenant community of Jonah's God, they are also 'lay' people. They are not religious professionals of any kind. But it is they who provide the example to follow. The fact that, in the story of God's people, this is so often the way of things, is worth thinking about. Why is it that, again and again, those who should know better, do not? And, if God is in control, why should he allow this to be? Does God, for some reason, want it like this?

There is a struggle here between omnipotence and the freedom required by perfect love. Such love will not let go, yet must not impose its will. On Calvary, the struggle comes to its climax. And almighty love prevails.

God of questioning,
in our struggle to follow you
help us to find you through your sovereign love.

Guidelines for groups (1)

Sharing together (25 mins)

1. If this is a new group, meeting for the first time, each person should take a moment to introduce themselves.

2. Share within the group any experience people have had of being asked to do something they did not want to do. How did it feel?

3. Each member of the group should say something of their hopes for your meetings together to discuss Jonah. Ask everyone to give their initial impressions from reading Jonah 1 and the study material. If you can, share one thing you gained and one question you bring.

4. If appropriate, outline something in your life that you have been reminded of by your study of Jonah 1. What was most significant about it? Did it change your way of thinking? Or your way of life?

Studying together (40 mins)

1. Not all Christians are called to be prophets. But we are all called to respond in some way to God's prompting. What do Jonah (and his fellow travellers) teach us about preparing ourselves to be open to God?

2. How easy is it for us to convince ourselves that we are doing what God wants? Are there ways in which we can learn to test our instincts?

3. What does the Book of Jonah teach us about God's providence?

4. Of the many questions posed in the text, which have struck home for you?

5. Where, for you, is the depth of God's love revealed in this passage?

Taking action together (10 mins)

1. Agree to take time each evening to reflect on how you have responded (or not) to God's promptings during the day.

2. Think of ways in which sharing the group's experiences in this way could strengthen your local church community.

Prayer together (15 mins)

1. First set the scene to allow the group to change gear. You may want to have a two-minute break, rearrange the chairs, or set up a visual focus for prayer such as an icon or candles.

2. Begin with a prayer asking for the Lord of the storm and the calm to be present with you. Follow this with a time of quiet: use either the silence or a piece of quiet music to allow hearts and minds to be still.

3. The leader should choose three or four key passages from Jonah 1, reading them slowly, leaving plenty of space between the chosen sections.

4. After you have pictured the scenes in your mind, imagine yourself as part of those on board the ship. What would you want God to be doing? What would you want to say to God? What might God be saying to you?

5. End with silence, music or a quiet song and a final prayer.

6. There may be things members want to note down in a journal or share with others. Go on reflecting on the passage, on your meditation, and on encountering the God of Jesus Christ, through the coming week.

Chapter 2
Out of the Deep – Jonah 2

A prayer poem

'Psalms and hymns and spiritual songs' (see Ephesians 5.19) have long been powerful vehicles for expressing prayer and communion with God. The Scriptures, both Hebrew and Christian, provide countless examples. There is a whole collection of them, of course, in the Book of Psalms. But they are to be found in many other biblical writings. Their music breaks through into prose narratives (see, for example, Exodus 15.1-21; Luke 1.46-55, 68-79) and characterizes many a prophetic word (for example, Isaiah 40 – 66; Jeremiah 10.12-16; 12.11-13; 14.1-10). Works such as Job and Lamentations are composed almost entirely in this medium. The second chapter of Jonah, therefore, is by no means an unusual phenomenon.

Poetry and music have a rare capacity to reach deep into the human soul. When they come together, as they do in psalms and laments, they can 'say' so much and evoke profound recognition. They can carry and give vent to the whole range of human experience and emotion – from exultation through to utter despair – and, in so doing, touch the heart of the matter. It is not surprising, then, that these biblical outpourings have become a primary resource for the prayer of the people of God. Whether or not we literally sing them, they are the soul's music. Plaintive, dissonant, exultant, upbeat, downbeat – whatever our condition, these prayer poems, again and again, strike just the right note.

That certainly seems to have been the case for Jesus. Steeped as he was in the spiritual heritage of the Jewish people, it was to psalms that he turned to bear his prayer at the time of his greatest crisis. 'My God, my God, why have you forsaken me?' he cries into the darkness of Calvary, echoing the desperate question of the psalmist at the opening of Psalm 22 (Mark 15.34; Psalm 22.1). And, as he yields his life to the mercy of a God he is determined to go on trusting, he draws from the depths the words of Psalm 31.5: 'Father, into your hands I commend my spirit' (Luke 23.46). Here, we should note the very significant addition Jesus makes to the original phrase from the psalm. After battling through the trauma of the crucifixion, he can again (and characteristically) call God 'Father'. Both these psalm prayers from the cross are sources of great encouragement for those who seek to hold to God in the midst of their own darkness.

At this stage in his journey, Jonah is undoubtedly in the dark. He has travelled from the hold of a ship to the belly of a fish. Both are places of confinement. In the first place, Jonah has hidden himself away from the tempest of the sea and the storm of his guilt. Now his place of security is provided by God. Safety is guaranteed. That he clearly senses. Yet, in his close confinement, he cannot see either the wider picture or the future course of things. He has no idea what will happen next. But he knows that, in an immediate sense at least, he has been delivered. The threat of the raging sea has been quelled. This can only be God's doing.

From this deep, yet safe darkness, Jonah turns at last to prayer and thanksgiving. What the mariners practised throughout the ordeal and beyond, Jonah now expresses from a strange sanctuary reminiscent of both tomb and womb. His striking prayer poem is sandwiched between two brief prose sections (v. 1 and v. 10), which are the contribution of the narrator. Through the prayer, Jonah is made to speak for himself in extended fashion. As we shall see, what he says is most revealing. It further fleshes out the character we have begun to get to know in the opening narrative. It shows us more of the redemptive sovereignty of God. And it points up the irony and fundamental significance of the whole story. Jonah's direct poetic speech also introduces a variety of style into the work, as well as suggesting something of the deeper meaning of what is going on.

It is sometimes said that this psalm-like section does not really belong to the story proper. The tale could be told without it. That much is true, of course. But, as suggested above, it is also the case that Jonah's prayer adds to the story dimensions it would otherwise lack. So it is, too, with a great narrative like that of the Book of Exodus. The punctuation of the narration by the song of triumph in Exodus 15 is not essential to the flow of the account, but it adds a flavour and a direction that enhance our appreciation of that formative act of deliverance.

In the Book of Jonah, whatever conclusion we might reach as to the poem's origins, it is now an integral part of the canonical book and we can gain much by engaging with it on those terms.

As Jonah's prayer rises from the belly of the fish, the ship and its sailors are left behind. But, in the intention of the narrator, their lessons most certainly are not. What we know as chapters one and two are connected episodes in the same drama. They both convey the same message: that the God who is universal in reach and operation is the God of sovereignty and grace. This message is the point of the whole work. In human terms, Jonah might be the character who appears in all the scenes, but it is God who is the major focus of attention, both centre stage and in the wings.

Through his rescue from the torrent of death, Jonah is being taught a lesson about the way God uses divine power. God works in even the most desperate of situations to bring salvation and new life. 'Deliverance belongs to the Lord,' as Jonah so rightly proclaims at the end of his prayer. The prophet's defiant disobedience, with all its terrifying consequences, has met nonetheless with merciful judgement. Jonah has been given personal experience of the truth God wants him to declare to the people of distant, sinful Nineveh. As it turns out, despite the fine words of his psalm-prayer, Jonah does not really learn the lesson of experience. He cannot make the connection between what happens to him and what God desires for those who, in Jonah's eyes, are undesirable aliens. Not even God can force Jonah to see divine sense.

Meanwhile, 'with the voice of thanksgiving' Jonah offers up his prayer. It follows the pattern of many a thanksgiving psalm (see, for example, Psalms 30 and 116). There is graphic representation of distress. There is a calling out to God for help. There is rejoicing that God comes to the rescue. And there are grateful pledges made to the God of deliverance. In the remainder of this chapter, we shall look more closely at these interweaving threads.

Lord, you put songs in our mouths:
cries, through fear of the unknown,
pleas, for deliverance from danger,
words of trust, in spite of our doubts,
a handing over to you, in spite of ourselves.

You who hear our words,
listen to what we really want to say.

Despair

Jonah's prayer poem articulates his despair in terms that are the stuff of nightmare. As we look particularly at verses 3-6a, we are given a vivid impression of someone overwhelmed by forces beyond his control, dragged under by that with which he cannot cope.

> You cast me into the deep,
>> into the heart of the seas,
>> and the flood surrounded me;
> all your waves and your billows
>> passed over me.
> Then I said, 'I am driven away
>> from your sight;
> how shall I look again
>> upon your holy temple?'
> The waters closed in over me;
>> the deep surrounded me;
> weeds were wrapped around my head
>> at the roots of the mountains.
> I went down to the land
>> whose bars closed upon me forever.

This is despair unto death. The imagery graphically conveys a sense of being inundated, inescapably trapped, pulled down into the eternal desolation of a deathly prison. It is an experience of awful finality. Adding pain upon pain, the experience brings with it a conviction of separation from God, of being driven from God's presence. Such a banishment can only bring utter hopelessness.

The poem describes Jonah's situation, but its portrayal of despair is readily applicable to so many others. At the hour of his death, even Jesus felt that God had forsaken him (Mark 15.34). The psalmists frequently cry out in this kind of extreme distress. Indeed, one such psalm includes exactly the phraseology used by Jonah:

> My soul is cast down within me . . .
> Deep calls to deep
>> at the thunder of your cataracts;
> all your waves and your billows
>> have gone over me.
>
> (Psalm 42.6-7)

Other psalmists, too, use drowning metaphors. Look, for example, at Psalm 69.1-2, 14-15. In Psalm 88, we encounter this:

> Your wrath lies heavy upon me,
>> and you overwhelm me with all your waves.
>
> (Psalm 88.7)

This last quotation points up a perspective that can only compound a feeling of despair. The psalmist believes that it is God who is doing the 'drowning' because of his displeasure. Jonah feels the same. It is God who has propelled him into the murky depths (v. 4). This is surely the consequence of his sin. Did not the mighty tempest say as much? But Jonah still has much to learn about the God who will not let him go. The waters of his 'tomb' will turn out to be a 'womb'; the 'bars' of his eternal prison but a gateway to new life. Disturbance wrought by God is creative and liberating in intent, though it bring severe travail. In the depths of his crisis, however, Jonah cannot see this truth. 'Going under' is the primary reality.

Countless people can identify with Jonah in this experience. For many, there is still a strong sense that their suffering is in some way a punishment from God. More often than not, this assumption becomes apparent through questioning and objection. 'Why is this happening to me (or to someone I love)?' 'I (or they) have done nothing to deserve this.' Such *cris de coeur* echo down the centuries. They are most certainly there in the biblical record.

Psalm 44 provides a good example of a whole people crying out to God. They accuse God of making them 'like sheep for slaughter' (v. 11) and of covering them with shame and disgrace.

Their approach could not be more direct. Desperation has made them bold. A keen sense of injustice has empowered them to dispense with reverential niceties. The same is true of one of the most high-profile individuals in distress to be found in the Bible – Job. Job endures disaster after disaster (Job 1 – 2). Yet he 'was blameless and upright, one who feared God and turned away from evil' (Job 1.1). Despite blow upon blow, Job persists in refusing to blame God (1.21; 2.10). But, eventually, even for Job such piety becomes untenable. After suffering in silence for seven days and seven nights, 'Job opened his mouth and cursed the day of his birth' (3.1). There is then unleashed a torrent of questioning and a repeated demand that God should both explain himself and allow Job to put his case directly to the Almighty. Job's determination is heightened by having to listen to several erstwhile friends telling him in various ways that he should stop objecting and accept that God is punishing him for his sin. In this, they are simply voicing conventional wisdom. That will not do for Job. His passionate representations pull no punches (see, for example, Job 16.6-17; 23.2-7).

In the end, Job gains not an audience in the divine court but a personal encounter with the living God. His refusal to accept theological generalities that he knows to be manifestly unfair opens the way for the God of deeper truth to get through.

And God leaves the 'theologically correct' friends in no doubt that they 'have not spoken of me what is right, as my servant Job has' (see 42.1-9). It seems, then, that raw honesty and frankness have God's blessing and are a healthy strategy to address deadly despair.

In terms of theological formulae, there is no easy answer to the ever-present question: 'What is the relationship between God and suffering?' We can say, certainly, that sin and wrongdoing have inevitable knock-on effects, which often affect 'innocent parties'. We can say that God is constantly working for good in all situations of suffering, whatever their provenance. But that will have to be an assertion of faith – particularly when we are being tossed around in pain's maelstrom. We can point to some interesting indicators in the Gospels. In John 9, for example, the disciples ask in relation to a man born blind, 'Rabbi, who sinned, this man or his parents, that he was born blind?' Jesus replies, 'Neither this man nor his parents sinned; he was born blind so that God's works might be revealed in him' (John 9.1-3). When Jesus' friend, Lazarus, falls ill, his first response is 'This illness . . . is for God's glory' (John 11.4). In Luke's Gospel, Jesus is recorded as saying, 'Those eighteen who were killed when the tower of Siloam fell on them – do you think that they were worse offenders than all the others living in Jerusalem? No, I tell you . . . ' (Luke 13.4-5).

Disability, illness, disaster – none of these is associated by Jesus with personal sin. Their causes lie elsewhere.

In pondering all these things, we are still left with many questions. They are beyond the power of our minds to comprehend neatly. If God really is God, then God must be beyond the scope of human intellect. But intellect is not all that God has given to humankind, precious though it be. There are relational and spiritual dimensions of being human that enable us to touch realities that defy argued definitions. Love is difficult to explain. It can, however, undoubtedly be experienced.

In this regard, the cross of Calvary is indeed the crux of the matter. Here, with the eyes of faith, we see the love of God *in extremis*. We see God, in Jesus, passionately struggling with suffering. We see God, in Jesus, bearing and redeeming the sin of the world. As Julian of Norwich put it in the fourteenth century, 'You would know our Lord's meaning in this thing? Know it well. Love was his meaning.'[1]

If we can hold to that insight, despair will not ultimately engulf us.

Lord, what are you doing to us?
Where are you taking us?
What do you want of us?
Dragged down as we are,
why have you forsaken us?

You who bear the ills of the world,
hear us from the depths of our being.

Prayer

Then Jonah prayed to the Lord his God from the belly
of the fish, saying,

'I called to the Lord out of my distress,
    and he answered me;
out of the belly of Sheol I cried,
    and you heard my voice . . .
As my life was ebbing away,
    I remembered the Lord;
and my prayer came to you,
    into your holy temple.'

(Jonah 2.1,2,7)

Desperation, at last, provokes Jonah to prayer. Only *in extremis*, when life itself
is all but lost, does he 'remember' the Lord. Utterly powerless to help himself, he
cries out to God. He does so as one who had told others to give him over to the
God of the storm (1.12). He had accepted that he, in his disobedience, should be
the placatory sacrifice he thought God required. When the deed is done, however,
the awful reality of the experience makes him cry out for dear life – not sacrificial
death. He was then to discover that God's 'wrath' is, in truth, a facet of divine
love. God does not come to destroy. God's passionate pursuit of Jonah is not to
make him a victim. It is to reclaim him as a partner in mission. It is in the interests
of his own well-being and that of countless others in Nineveh. If there is anger in
God's love, it is because what is good and life-embracing has been jeopardized.
Even in hot dismay, God works to redeem situations and to draw out from them
any potential they might have for good. Many a human parent will recognize this
phenomenon. Again and again, God displays it to perfection.

Jonah, of course, should have known better. He should have known God better. Even now, after such a dramatic experience of salvation, it will become apparent that Jonah is still slow (or unwilling) to learn God's lessons. So it was with the first disciples of Jesus. So it was, and is, with so many of God's servants. God's understandable exasperation is well reflected in some words of Jesus recorded in Mark's Gospel (9.19): 'You faithless generation, how much longer must I be among you? How much longer must I put up with you?' Yet, 'put up with' us God does. Jonah is not a special case. At all times and in all places, 'the steadfast love of the Lord never ceases' (Lamentations 3.22). The most abject failures in discipleship meet with mercy. Good Friday and Easter are our guarantee of that, as the experience of the apostles so powerfully testified. Having run away, they hid away – but God's forgiveness, peace and new commissioning found them out (see John 20.19-23). In this respect, too, Jonah is a prefiguring of their story.

Before he turns to address God directly, Jonah begins his prayer poem with a statement that encapsulates (and bears witness to) the response of God to a distress call: 'he answered me'. That is a message that not only God needs to hear! It is an experience proclaimed in testimony by many other scriptural psalms. Some are worthy of particular reflection because their imagery is so consonant with Jonah's prayer. The composer of Psalm 18 expresses it like this:

> The cords of death encompassed me;
>> the torrents of perdition assailed me;
> the cords of Sheol entangled me;
>> the snares of death confronted me.
>
> In my distress I called upon the Lord;
>> to my God I cried for help.
> From his temple he heard my voice,
>> and my cry to him reached his ears.
>
> (Psalm 18.4-6)

Here is someone who, like Jonah, is helplessly trapped and going under. This psalmist, too, speaks of Sheol as the inescapable place of death. In the cultural understanding of the time Sheol was the abode of the dead. It was also frequently known as 'the Pit' (see Jonah's prayer at v. 6), which conveys the sense that death is a descent into fathomless darkness. The pit of Sheol is the place of no hope, where shadowy spirits are held in thrall. As such, it is no place for God. That belief is well summarized in Psalm 88:

> Do you work wonders for the dead?
> > Do the shades rise up to praise you?
> Is your steadfast love declared in the grave,
> > or your faithfulness in Abaddon?
> Are your wonders known in the darkness,
> > or your saving help in the land of forgetfulness?
>
> > > (Psalm 88.10-12)

This psalmist clearly expects the answer 'no'. He is not alone; not just in his own cultural setting but among many who have come after. Death seems to be the final frontier, which all but God can cross. 'The rest is silence', as Shakespeare put it (in *Hamlet*). Yet God strives to break through with a far more positive message – to which Jonah's deliverance from death is a striking pointer. Jonah, like so many others, discovers that God's wonders are most certainly known in the dark. God's saving help reaches into the ultimate depths. Just as there is nowhere on earth where God cannot operate, so the territory of death lies open to his redeeming love. That becomes abundantly clear when we look to Jesus. For the Son of God, 'the Pit' was the opposite of a no-go area. In the bitter crisis of death, it became the place of his visitation: 'He descended into hell' (Apostles' Creed; see also 1 Peter 3.18-20). However deep our darkness, 'God knows'. And we can know, in faith, that God's steadfast love is declared in the grave. The outcome is resurrection life – 'indescribable and glorious joy' (1 Peter 1.9).

Jonah's story is an indicator of this profound truth. In despair and terror he cries out to God from 'the belly of Sheol', from the grim confines of hopelessness. His voice is heard, and Jonah expresses his rejoicing to 'the Lord his God'. God's answer is to transfer Jonah to 'the belly of the fish'. Still confined, but safe and sound, he now awaits 'delivery' into a new phase of life. The darkness has changed its tone. It is suffused with hope. Death is not the master. God is.

Prayer reaches out after this reality. That is not only the case, of course, with those for whom prayer is a customary activity. Far from it. 'When other helpers fail', and *in extremis*, even the most cynical and irreligious find themselves calling out to God – if only by uttering God's name. God by no means despises such selective 'remembrance'. It is both sought after and welcomed. 'Out of the depths I cry to you, O Lord. Lord hear my voice!' (Psalm130.1) is a *cri de coeur* that goes straight to the heart of God. And not a few have found that meeting God in the depths has been a turning point in their whole lives. When things are at their worst, truth is exposed.

So Jonah realized. He gives thanks to God that his prayer 'came to you, into your holy temple' (v. 7). For the people of God in Jonah's time, the Temple was the focus of God's presence. Located in Jerusalem, it was the centre of pilgrimage and sacrificial worship. The inner sanctum, or holy of holies, was believed to be the special dwelling place of God's glory. As such, only the High Priest was allowed to enter it, and he but once a year (on the Day of Atonement) after elaborate rites of purification. The unholy could not survive in a context of such burning purity. With such a perception, the distance between the belly of Sheol and the heart of the Temple must seem an all but unbridgeable chasm. Jonah discovers, however, that honest prayer bridges the gap. What he has still to learn is that the 'gap' is a human construction. Just as God will not be limited to a particular building, city or land, nor will God's holiness keep him apart from a beloved creation, either in life or death. The desire of holy love is always for communion, not separation. God's 'temple' is everywhere – and the door is always open. What awaits is gracious welcome, not summary destruction.

A fitting response to this must surely be thanksgiving and the offering of praise. Even Jonah, finally, connects with this response:

> I with the voice of thanksgiving
>> will sacrifice to you;
> what I have vowed I will pay.

(Jonah 2.9)

Saying 'thank you' to God must rejoice his heart. At our best, we human beings give help to others for their own sake and because they need it, not to gain thanks. But the bonus of thanksgiving does bring joy. How much more so with God. If God enters fully into our misery, shall we deny him the sharing of our joy? On our part, too, thanksgiving enlarges our understanding of God's love and opens us more deeply to it. It speaks through our self-centredness. It is our duty and our joy.

In the initial flush of relief and euphoria, promises are often made to the one who has brought saving help. They are less frequently delivered as the passage of time dulls remembrance of the intensity of the experience. Jonah's subsequent behaviour strongly suggests that this was the case with him. Certainly, if he vowed obedience, it was only grudgingly put into practice. In terms of relating to God, Jonah's memory proves lamentably short.

Meanwhile, on the surface of the water, the sailors who consigned Jonah to the deep also make vows (1.16). We cannot help suspecting that they will be rather more ready to keep their promises with a good heart.

> Hear us, Lord, in the midst of our darkness.
> Untangle the confused threads of life,
> and put us together again,
> that we may fulfil our vows,
> not only with our lips but with our lives.
>
> You who hold all things in your hand,
> deliver us that we may live for you.

God's response

> Out of the belly of Sheol I cried,
>   and you heard my voice.
> . . . you brought up my life from the Pit . . .
>   Deliverance belongs to the Lord!

(Jonah 2.2,6,9)

Jonah's God is a merciful Saviour. Just as (as *The Book of Common Prayer* puts it) God's 'property is always to have mercy', so rescuing from dire despair is integral to God's character and ministry. Deliverance *belongs* to the Lord in the sense that it is proper to God's nature. It is an expression of what God is like. Deliverance also belongs to the Lord in the sense that it is *God's* work. Whatever agents God might work with and through, fundamentally it is God who effects salvation. God's mission is always to save: to bring out the best, to work things together for good.

In Jonah's case, we could say that God rises to a considerable challenge! Until the moment of ultimate crisis, Jonah is hardly cooperative. Yet when, at last, he cries out to God in fear and helplessness, God takes decisive action. Jonah is delivered. His rescue is a classic illustration of a key truth: that, in God's perspective, salvation does not depend upon worthiness to be saved. The need is all. Yet there is another significant factor – not worthiness but willingness. However faintly, the one in need has to want to be saved. We know from human experience how difficult it is to help those who refuse to accept help, either because they do not recognize their need or have become so wedded to it that 'divorce' is unthinkable. Sometimes this is due to an all-consuming conviction of not 'deserving' deliverance. With all such attitudes God struggles to get through; to expose the truth of crying human need and divine determination to save. The smallest sign of recognition creates an opening for God. The Lord to whom deliverance belongs is not slow to seize opportunities. However, forcing salvation on anyone is not God's way. That would critically undermine the Creator's precious gift of free will.

So God did not stop Jonah running away – and into trouble. But God is quick to respond when Jonah cries to him 'out of the belly of Sheol', from the depths of 'the Pit'. There is something of a parallel here with Jesus' parable of the Prodigal Son (Luke 15.11-32). In engaging with the issues of worthiness and willingness, this is a most fruitful story to contemplate. The father sees his son and rushes out to him while he is 'still far off'. The son does not have to make all the running! But he does have to come to himself before he is capable of receiving joyful restoration.

It is the imminent prospect of being swallowed up by the Pit that brings Jonah to his senses. He quickly discovers that, as Julian of Norwich put it back in the fourteenth century, God reaches down 'to our most lowly needs'.[2] God meets him in the depths to which he has sunk, in a place where there seems to be no escape. The cry of despair is readily heard. The darkness of death is robbed of its prey. But emergence into the light of new life is not immediate. There is further confinement in the belly of the fish. Here, trust is of the essence – believing God has come to the rescue, when the outcome is not at all clear.

Looked at from a human perspective, God's way of delivering is not always straightforward or easy to understand. That is certainly the case with God's focal act of salvation in Jesus Christ. Why did God choose the way of the Cross? It surely did not have to be like this. According to Matthew's Gospel, on the night Jesus was arrested, he said to that companion who would defend him by force, 'Put your sword back in its place; for all who take the sword will perish by the sword. Do you think that I cannot appeal to my Father, and he will at once send me more than twelve legions of angels? But how then would the scriptures be fulfilled, which say it must happen in this way?' (Matthew 26.52-54). God will not impose deliverance by the use of superior force. That would be domination, not true deliverance. It would not reach the heart of the matter, the profundity of human need. Neither would that be achieved by a mere closing of God's eyes to the effects of sin, suffering and evil. Taking salvation seriously meant that it had to be, so to speak, 'an inside job' – 'in Christ God was reconciling the world to himself' (2 Corinthians 5.19). Through the horror that Jesus went through on the cross, we can be assured that God shares our darkness and pain, that God knows (literally) what it can mean to live and die in a world where all is not well. That this is so means that the saving mercy of God connects directly with our worst experiences and with the least attractive side of human nature. Through the passion of love, God faces head-on all that makes for destruction.

And, for a time, it seemed as if all were lost. Just as Jonah was hidden in the belly of the fish for three days and three nights, so the crucified Jesus lay hidden in the tomb. Only on the third day, 'while it was still dark', did he burst out of this deadly enfolding. Through Christ's resurrection we are shown, in more ways than one, that death has had its day. Jonah's story is but a faint echo of this great truth.

God's deliverance of Jonah is nonetheless dramatic: 'Then the Lord spoke to the fish, and it spewed Jonah out upon the dry land' (2.10). A somewhat humiliating experience for one of God's prophets! Yet he has been saved. God has preserved his life, if not his dignity. It is worth recalling at this point that God has delivered Jonah by working in partnership with a representative of non-human creation, with a fish. It is indicative of humanity's tendency to arrogance that, even in a faith context, we so often fail to acknowledge the significance to God (and ourselves) of the rest of creation. We do so to our sore loss and, indeed, at our peril.

In this case, Jonah could have learnt much from his host, the fish, about responding to God's prompting. By contrast to Jonah, the fish carries out God's orders with immediate and unquestioning obedience. Fortunately for a rebellious, human prophet, God can rely on this creature of the deep.

God of deliverance,
thank you for setting us free.
Uphold us lest we fall back,
and be with us as we journey on,
that we may be free to do your will.

You who bring life out of death,
draw us into your mission of love.

Pride and prejudice

> Those who worship vain idols
> forsake their true loyalty.
> But I with the voice of thanksgiving
> will sacrifice to you.
>
> (Jonah 2.8-9)

Jonah's experience of deliverance points to the fact that the God of mercy is disposed to forgive rather than to punish. Though the psalm-poem we are pondering largely seems to grasp this, the one through whose mouth it is spoken evidently does not. He can neither see nor accept that the God who saves sinner Jonah might also be prepared to save sinners from other backgrounds and cultures. Even in his prayer, Jonah cannot let go of his prejudice or his self-centredness.

These aspects of his personality and behaviour come through loud and clear in the whole of the Jonah narrative. Jonah is first and foremost concerned with himself. It is his situation, his feelings, and his perception of things that really matter. They should, therefore, be God's priorities as well. And when God does not oblige, Jonah 'punishes' him by running away, arguing and sulking. It is a very childish approach in an adult prophet. But it is, of course, an approach by no means confined to Jonah. The temptation to expect that God should fit in with our wishes and our view is a strong one, and ever with us. We want our own way, and we work on the assumption that God should see the world in the same way that we do. When God attempts to broaden our horizons, we all too often react negatively and object petulantly. When it comes to relating to God, there is something of Jonah in all of us.

Jonah's self-preoccupation is reflected in the preponderance of the first person singular throughout his contribution to the narrative. Again and again, he speaks in terms of 'I' and 'me'. That is certainly the case with his extended prayer. Appropriate though this may be in giving thanks for personal deliverance, it is nonetheless indicative of Jonah's fundamental emphasis. We notice, for example, that the focus of the prayer is not so much praise of God, as the nature of Jonah's plight. Indeed, 'the voice of thanksgiving' is relegated to the very end of the prayer – as is the exclamation that 'Deliverance belongs to the Lord!' The example provided by Jonah should act as a salutary caution against a spirituality that centres on self. In this regard, it might perhaps be healthy to review on a regular basis the prayers, hymns and songs that we use. How dominant is the first-person singular? What is our language saying about the state and inclination of our soul?

In Jonah's case, his self-centredness goes hand in hand with self-righteousness and judgemental prejudice. Even when celebrating his own rescue, he still manages to take the opportunity to find fault with others:

> Those who worship vain idols
>   forsake their true loyalty.

(Jonah 2.8)

And immediately he contrasts such reprehensible idolatry with the purity of his own spiritual conduct:

> But I with the voice of thanksgiving
>   will sacrifice to you.

(Jonah 2.9)

To use colloquial language, this really is a bit rich! Jonah is speaking of a matter where, to say the least, he has something of a beam in his own eye (see Matthew 7.3). What else has Jonah done than 'forsake his true loyalty' by trying to run away from God? As for 'those who worship vain idols', be they pagan sailors or Ninevites, they can give Jonah lessons in honouring his God.

Again, Jonah is far from alone in displaying such unself-critical prejudice. It runs like a dark thread through the Scriptures, often weaving a pattern of violence and destruction. Not infrequently, those considered beyond the boundaries of acceptability are marginalized, excluded or destroyed – be they external enemies or internal misfits. Often this is done under the conviction that God requires it. Many of the Psalms are redolent with this fierce (and vengeful) sense of righteousness (see, for example, Psalms 21.8-12; 75; 79; 83; 137.7-9; 139.19-22).

Yet this is most certainly not the whole picture. The Bible also presents us with a broader and deeper perspective. This is highlighted, not least, by the Book of Jonah and its message. If God created all things (Jonah 1.9), God also cares about all things, desiring their welfare, not their condemnation (for example, 4.10,11). Sin and 'disloyalty' are not to be condoned but, as far as God is concerned, they are to be redeemed. And God's redeeming love is offered to all.

Such is the message of the gospel. As proclaimed and lived by Jesus, it brought about a focal clash of perspectives. How could this man who consorted with sinners and sat loose to religious law be truly a messenger of the holy God? How could it be that, as this man claimed, God loved and wanted relationship with even those outside the holy community of the chosen? Surely this was dangerous delusion. For the good of God's people, it must be eliminated. And so to Calvary.

It is tragic irony that, as in this crucial instance, so often throughout history passionate commitment to what is believed to be God's cause has resulted in suffering and bloodshed. Religious wars and persecution have stained the name of God and cut short so many human lives. When we are tempted (as Jesus puts it at Luke 18.9) to trust in ourselves that we are righteous and to condemn others, we should recall where such attitudes can lead. We are all in need of God's mercy. None of us is qualified to play God. As in Jonah's case, those who see matters of faith and spirituality differently from us may have riches to share with us – riches that are, in fact, from God's many-splendoured treasury. To put it another way, God does not only speak to us through what we might regard as 'authorized channels'. As with the coming of Jesus, God's encounters with us can take us by surprise. How we respond makes all the difference.

The essence of the matter is God's saving love. The Jonah narrative seeks to get this across. The writer of Colossians fleshes it out:

> For in Christ all the fullness of God was pleased to
> dwell, and through him God was pleased to reconcile
> to himself all things, whether on earth or in heaven,
> by making peace through the blood of his cross.
>
> (Colossians 1.19,20)

No other bloodshedding is needed, either literal or metaphorical. And there is no greater love.

Lord of all the world,
let the 'I' of my concern
become the 'me' that others see,
that we may reach beyond our self-interest
to appreciate the glories of those around us.

You who take pride in the variety of your creation,
wipe away our prejudice and set us free.

Liberation

> 'Deliverance belongs to the Lord!'
> Then the Lord spoke to the fish, and it spewed Jonah
> out upon the dry land.
>
> (Jonah 2.9-10)

In a rather startling way, Jonah experiences the truth of his prayer acclamation. Powerless to set himself free, he now knows the ministry of God as liberator. By the grace of God and the obedient cooperation of the fish, Jonah is delivered from his confinement in the fish's belly. Out of that tomb/womb, and back on dry land, he should now be a 'born again' prophet, ready to do God's will. As we know, however, evidence for a new beginning proves sketchy, at best. Liberation by the Lord does not seem to convince Jonah that to serve God is perfect freedom.

So it was with the people of Israel after their liberation from slavery in Egypt. In the Passover and the Exodus, they experienced, through the working of God, a great act of deliverance from a desperate and destructive situation. It was a defining moment, both in terms of their identity as a people and by its decisive revelation of God's nature as saviour. So it became a 'moment' to be remembered and celebrated, year after year, in a major religious festival – that of Passover. The reason for rejoicing is well summed up in two verses from Exodus 3:

> Then the Lord said, 'I have observed the misery of
> my people who are in Egypt; I have heard their cry
> on account of their taskmasters. Indeed, I know their
> sufferings, and I have come down to deliver them
> from the Egyptians, and to bring them up out of that
> land to a good and broad land, a land flowing with
> milk and honey . . .'
>
> (Exodus 3.7-8)

God sees, hears, knows – and acts to save.

Yet the liberated ones were soon murmuring their discontent and complaints. The 'good and broad land' seemed a long way off. The going was tough. Perhaps, after all, they'd been better off in Egypt. They were not prepared, it seems, to journey trustfully with the One who had wrested them from tyranny. Though God's saving power and commitment to them had been so dramatically demonstrated, they wanted their liberated pilgrimage to be on their own terms – their 'milk and honey' supplied to order.

Jonah displays the same trait. If we are honest, so do we all. Our memories and our trust tend to be short term. We are happy for God to rescue us. But, afterwards, we are all too often inclined to expect God to service our freedom according to our agenda and timings. Or we begin to doubt God's goodwill and love, even when there is striking previous evidence to bring to bear. Fortunately for us, God still sees and hears and knows – and acts to save. That is the way God is. Neither our grumbling nor our lack of faith will cause God to change his ways, to abandon his loving purpose.

If we want proof of that, we need only look to God's greatest act of liberation accomplished, significantly, at the time of the Feast of Passover. It is no accident that what God did on Good Friday and Easter Sunday came to be understood as a new Exodus – the ultimate deliverance from the slavery of sin and the bondage of death. As St Paul puts it to the Christians in Corinth, 'For our paschal lamb, Christ, has been sacrificed. Therefore, let us celebrate the festival' (1 Corinthians 5.7,8). This time it was not a lamb that suffered. It was God's own Son. Here, indeed, is a strange mystery. There were many at that time looking for God's Messiah to liberate them from the occupying power of the Roman Empire. What actually happened when Christ Jesus fulfilled his ministry broke the bounds of all expectation. That God's Son should effect salvation by dying a disgraceful death, with forgiveness on his lips, defied all understanding. It still does. But only this inexplicable love can truly set us free.

Free, therefore, to join thankfully with God in his mission of love. That may well prove costly on all sorts of levels, but it is labour that gives birth to the profoundest joy. Knowing we are loved at all times and in all places by One who gives his life for us, should fire us to make that love known to others. For this is also the One through and for whom all things have been created, and in whom all things hold together (Colossians 1.16,17). The power of the universe is characterized by sacrificial love.

Jonah did not know of Calvary, but he knew (with his head at least) that God had created all things (1.9). He also knew for himself the power of God's saving love. Yet making the connection with God's desire to save distant Nineveh seems beyond him. It was in his own interests to accept that God was at liberty to deliver him from destruction. He was, to say the least, reluctant to allow God the freedom so to act in relation to those he considered heathen outsiders.

Jonah has been brought back to where he started. It seems he is only a little wiser for all he has gone through. But God has not finished with him yet.

In the midst of life we experience death,
yet you, our God, deliver us.
Transform our attitudes to others,
that we may rejoice with those who rejoice,
and weep with those who weep.

You who bring us out of our prisons,
set us free to do your will.

Guidelines for groups (2)

Sharing together (30 mins)

1. Briefly update each other on the outcome of actions agreed at the last meeting.

2. Ask everyone to give their initial impressions from reading Jonah 2 and the study material. If you can, share one thing you gained and one question you bring.

3. Share any experience you've had of praying in a crisis.

Studying together (40 mins)

1. Jesus expressed telling prayers through his use of Scripture. Do we? Can we learn from Jonah more about this way of praying? Can we use it to enrich corporate worship?

2. Are our church communities honest enough to express despair, as well as petition and praise, in their corporate worship? How might we use Jonah to help them in this?

3. What might we learn from Jonah about vows and promises?

4. 'The fish carries out God's orders.' Do we?

5. What most surprises you in this chapter? And what do you find hardest to take?

Taking action together (10 mins)

1. Find ways of expressing, through corporate prayer, what you have learned from Jonah about ways of praying.

2. How can we help those in our church communities who feel trapped and overwhelmed by their circumstances?

Prayer together (20 mins)

1. First set the scene to allow the group to change gear. You may want to have a two-minute break, rearrange the chairs, or set up a visual focus for prayer such as an icon or candles.

2. Begin with a prayer asking for the God of liberation to be present with you. Follow this with a time of quiet: use either the silence or a piece of quiet music to allow hearts and minds to be still.

3. The leader should choose two or three key verses from Jonah 2, reading them slowly, leaving plenty of space between the chosen sections.

4. After you have pictured the scenes in your mind, imagine yourself as the fish, and then as Jonah. What would you want to ask of God? What might God be saying to you?

5. End with silence, music or a quiet song and a final prayer.

6. There may be things members want to note down in a journal or share with others. Go on reflecting on the passage, on your meditation, and on encountering the God of Jesus Christ through the coming week.

Chapter 3
Mission Accomplished – Jonah 3

The second time of asking (3.1-4)

> The word of the Lord came to Jonah a second time,
> saying, 'Get up, go to Nineveh, that great city, and
> proclaim to it the message that I tell you.' So Jonah set
> out and went to Nineveh, according to the word of the
> Lord. Now Nineveh was an exceedingly large city, a
> three days' walk across. Jonah began to go into the
> city, going a day's walk. And he cried out, 'Forty days
> more, and Nineveh shall be overthrown!'

The Lord does not give up easily. The welfare of those who are turning away from what is good means too much to him. Dealing with Jonah's obduracy has delayed things, but now the mission must be accomplished. Matters are urgent. Jonah is therefore given his marching orders a second time. The way in which God's command is expressed suggests that Jonah is given very little time for recuperation after being 'spewed out' on the shore. 'Get up,' says God, and go and do my bidding. No further time is to be lost or wasted. Jonah can come to terms with his recent personal drama in the carrying out of God's will. Perhaps through that he will more thoroughly learn his lesson. Jonah's needs have been well attended to. At this point, the needs of the Ninevites take priority.

Jonah is now facing one of those divine imperatives that cut through to the heart of the matter and require an immediate response. When God says, 'Get up and go' in this manner, those addressed are presented with a critical choice. One way or another, they must act. And, invariably, these key moments of decision have major implications for others as well as themselves. Among many examples in the Scriptures, we may recall the case of Abraham, the 'founder member', as it were, of God's chosen people. We read in Genesis 12 how the Lord said to him, 'Go from your country and your kindred and your father's house to the land that I will show you.' There was a promise attached to this order to journey into the unknown: 'I will make of you a great nation, and I will bless you and . . . you will be a blessing.' Abraham's response is succinctly put: 'So Abram went, as the Lord had told him.' As the Letter to the Hebrews later puts it, 'By faith . . . he set out, not knowing where he was going' (Hebrews 11.8). His faithful obedience was momentous in its consequences. It set in train the pilgrimage of a whole community of faith.

At a crucial point in that pilgrimage, God visited his people in the person of Jesus. In infancy, the life of Jesus was threatened by a power-obsessed king, Herod. Matthew's Gospel tells us that 'an angel of the Lord appeared to Joseph in a dream and said, "Get up, take the child and his mother, and flee to Egypt, and remain there until I tell you; for Herod is about to search for the child, to destroy him"' (Matthew 2.13). Had Joseph not obeyed, the course of salvation history might have been very different. As it was, the bloodshedding and pain of Calvary was prefigured in Herod's massacre of the innocents (Matthew 2.16-18).

Later, another persecutor was first brought to his knees and then told to get up and go. On the road to Damascus, Saul of Tarsus had his whole life dramatically turned round (Acts 9.1-30). From 'breathing threats and murder against the disciples of the Lord' he began boldly to proclaim Jesus as the Son of God. We know him as Paul the Apostle, formative figure in the life and development of the Early Church, whose continuing influence over the centuries has been immense. And all because he was not 'disobedient to the heavenly vision' (Acts 26.19).

Paul's example highlights a vital spiritual truth. With God, no one is dismissed as a lost cause – however much damage they are doing. The early Christians found that difficult to believe about Saul of Tarsus (Acts 9.26). Jonah found it difficult to believe about the people of Nineveh. We, too, can find it hard to credit. Understandably so, in human terms. But God's ways are not our ways. God is not only merciful to sinners. He labours to draft them in as co-workers in building up the kingdom. When we examine our own, less than pure, hearts, we may have added reason to be thankful for that.

Whether Jonah was truly thankful is a moot point. Apparently, however, he has rediscovered his capacity to obey. Off he goes at last to an alien culture, to the centre of an unfriendly foreign power. Recalling the threat posed to God's covenant people by the mighty Assyria in its heyday, we can perhaps begin to imagine what a journey Jonah had to undertake – in terms of attitude and spiritual understanding as well as physical distance. As Christ was later to make painfully clear, even enemies have to be loved. God's love crosses all boundaries – and so must the messengers of that love. For the real possibility of a change of heart must be made known to all. As God was trying to impress upon Jonah, such repentance, such deep-down change, such turning in God's direction, is equally required of those within the community of faith, as well as those considered outside (and against) it. 'Them' and 'us' are not appropriate vocabulary for servants of God. Together, we are all constantly being called to open ourselves to the challenge of God's searching love. Who, except God, knows where that might lead us?

> God of persistence,
> help us to respond to your nagging call,
> to go out for you in spite of our doubts,
> to trust you though others let us down,
> to put aside fear and to rest in your strength.
>
> You who go on calling us to your work,
> strengthen our will to respond.

Message received (3.5-6)

> And the people of Nineveh believed God; they
> proclaimed a fast, and everyone, great and small,
> put on sackcloth.
>
> When the news reached the king of Nineveh, he rose
> from his throne, removed his robe, covered himself
> with sackcloth, and sat in ashes.

Like the seamen, the elements and the fish, the great city of Nineveh proves more responsive than Jonah to the word of the Lord. Jonah had only covered a third of the area designated for his preaching tour (a day's walk in a city that was 'three days' walk across') when very positive results become apparent. The whole community, struck by the truth of God's message, goes into 'repentance mode'. Lifestyle is abruptly changed. Self-denial takes over from self-indulgence. And this radical response involves everyone, both 'great and small'. The phrase is a comprehensive one, embracing all social classes and all ages. Soon the animals, too, will be included (vv. 7-8). Jonah could scarcely have expected such an immediate and wholehearted reaction from a foreign city whose wickedness had come up before God (1.2).

The message they so clearly heard and received was a stark, yet ambiguous one (whether in the Hebrew or Assyrian language). 'Forty days more, and Nineveh shall be overthrown!' Such was the word the Lord had commanded Jonah to speak (3.1,4). How was it to be understood? The threat was clear enough, but was its execution inevitable? And who was issuing this threat? Its mouthpiece was evidently some kind of divine prophet. His words had the ring of a deity about them. And they struck home. But they also made clear that judgement had been deferred for 'forty days'. Forty was commonly used in the ancient Near East to denote a significant number (a good many) rather than a precise figure. It was also often associated with a time of testing and purging (so, for example, the Israelites' forty years of wandering in the wilderness after the Exodus, and the forty days and nights of testing Jesus spent in the desert at the outset of his ministry). The people of Nineveh interpreted the forty days proclaimed by Jonah as the provision of an opportunity to repent. They lost no time in grasping that opportunity. Better be safe than sorry. They would also have heard the double meaning in the last word of the message. It could mean both 'overthrow' and 'change of heart'. They obviously wanted to be sure that it was the latter sense of the word that was realized. Their discernment was quick and acute. Here was a divine message offering two possibilities, each of which was to be taken with equal seriousness. In relation to both, they 'believed God'. Either they could await the disaster of God's judgement or they 'could turn from their wickedness and live'. In their hearing and their response, the Ninevites are exemplary. Yet they are 'heathen outsiders'.

Such outsiders seem to have a biblical track record in setting an example. That is certainly the case in relation to the life and ministry of Jesus. On not a few occasions, Jesus pointed up how much could be learnt from those not thought to belong. In one of his most famous parables (recorded at Luke 10.30-37) he chose a despised Samaritan as the character who practised mercy and was, therefore, to be emulated. 'Go and do likewise' said Jesus to the self-righteous lawyer who had prompted the story. Later in Luke's Gospel, we learn that, after Jesus has healed ten lepers (themselves all marginalized because of their disease), only one of them returns to give thanks. 'And he was a Samaritan' (Luke 17.16). The response of Jesus is telling: 'Was none of them found to return and give praise to God except this foreigner?' In Matthew's Gospel we learn of a Gentile centurion who displays such trust in Jesus that Jesus says of him, 'Truly I tell you, in no one in Israel have I found such faith' (Matthew 8.5-13).

And, at the climax of the Gospel story, it is another centurion (one who in the course of his duty has been instrumental in putting Jesus to death) who perceives the real truth about this crucified outcast. 'Truly,' he declares, 'this man was God's son' (Mark 15.39). He is not even a disciple, yet his insight penetrates the darkness.

The people of Nineveh stand in an honourable, if surprising, tradition. That includes their king. When he becomes aware of Jonah's message and the people's response, he lays aside his royal dignity, exchanging his royal robe for sackcloth and ashes. These are standard symbols of repentance, mourning and grief – the physical discomfort they involve expressive of a far deeper inner distress.

Again, the irony is heavy. An enemy ruler, an 'unbeliever', shows how leadership under God should be exercised. The kings of Israel and Judah could (for the most part) hardly boast in this regard. We can see a particular contrast between Nineveh and Jerusalem in the behaviour of King Jehoiakim of Judah (609–598 BC). In the fourth year of Jehoiakim's reign, the prophet Jeremiah is told by God to write on a scroll a collection of all the words of warning he has been given to communicate thus far. 'It may be', says God, 'that when the house of Judah hears of all the disasters I intend to do to them, all of them may turn from their evil ways, so that I may forgive their iniquity and their sin' (Jeremiah 36.3). When the people hear the scroll read they proclaim 'a fast before the Lord'. When their king listens to it, however, the outcome is rather different. 'As Jehudi read three or four columns, the king would cut them off with a penknife and throw them into the fire in the brazier, until the entire scroll was consumed in the fire . . .' (Jeremiah 36.9,23). He was soon to reap the reward of his arrogant faithlessness (see 2 Kings 24.1-5).

The king of Nineveh 'rose from his throne . . . and sat in ashes'. That act of penitent humility was impressive enough. But his action did not stop there. For this ruler, response had to connect with responsibility. He now, therefore, gives a further lead to his people.

God of justice,
speak your word of warning
until we admit our faults and change our ways.
Give us time and space,
but not too much.

You who go on calling us to account,
strengthen our will to repent.

Message understood (3.7-9)

> Then he had a proclamation made in Nineveh: 'By the
> decree of the king and his nobles: No human being or
> animal, no herd or flock, shall taste anything. They
> shall not feed, nor shall they drink water. Human
> beings and animals shall be covered with sackcloth,
> and they shall cry mightily to God. All shall turn from
> their evil ways and from the violence that is in their
> hands. Who knows? God may relent and change his
> mind; he may turn from his fierce anger, so that we do
> not perish.'

For the king of Nineveh, radical personal response combines with a sense of
responsibility for the entire city and all that is in it. Effective action is taken.
An official decree is issued calling all to forsake what is wrong, to show clear
signs of repentance and to cry 'mightily' to God for mercy.

This is certainly a no holds barred approach to repentance. As far as fasting is
concerned, even water is forbidden. They are to hunger and thirst for God's mercy,
physically as well as spiritually, in an extreme way. Fasting, as an expression of
in-depth prayer, is to be found throughout the biblical record. It is associated
particularly with penitence, grief, intensive intercession, profound commitment
and the search for discernment. So Jesus fasted for forty days and forty nights in
the wilderness (Matthew 4.2). The early Christians at Antioch perceived the
leading of the Holy Spirit 'while they were worshipping the Lord and fasting'
(Acts 13.2,3, see also Acts 14.23). In earlier times, Daniel 'turned to the Lord
God, to seek an answer by prayer and supplication with fasting and sackcloth
and ashes' (Daniel 9.3). When Nehemiah, in exile, heard of the shameful and
ruinous state of Jerusalem, he sat down and wept, and mourned for days, fasting
and praying before the God of heaven (Nehemiah 1.4). The psalmist graphically
portrays the physical effects that can accompany the extreme practice of this
spiritual discipline. Lamenting the fact that he is ridiculed for it he says:

> My knees are weak through fasting;
> my body has become gaunt.

> (Psalm 109.24)

We find a particularly interesting parallel with the Nineveh fast in Joel chapter 2 (see especially vv. 11-29). Here, it is God's covenant people who are exhorted to return to God 'with fasting, with weeping, and with mourning' (v. 12). This penitential fast is to include everyone, 'even infants at the breast' (v. 16). And it is to be accompanied by urgent and earnest prayer:

> Spare your people, O Lord,
>   and do not make your heritage a mockery,
>   a byword among the nations.

> (Joel 2.17)

Fasting is intended to mark a turning away from self-centredness in order to be more acutely open to God. It signals, in a way that is costly, the desire to renounce evil and to make obedience to God the absolute priority. It acknowledges and submits to God's sovereignty in the midst of sin or sorrow. It looks, therefore, for mercy and guidance – for God's sovereignty is the sovereignty of grace. Yet, like all that has potential for good, the practice of fasting can be misused. It can work against the healthy purpose for which it was intended. It can become an empty ritual, because it is devoid of any serious moral and spiritual commitment. It can degenerate into an exhibitionism born of a self-satisfied spirituality. Jesus had some sharp words to say about this (see Matthew 6.16-18), pointing to the essence of the matter in one of his soul-piercing sound bites:

> Not everyone who says to me, 'Lord, Lord,' will enter
> the kingdom of heaven, but only the one who does the
> will of my Father in heaven.

> (Matthew 7.21)

Any repentance that fasting represents must be a matter of the heart and result in behaviour that befits a genuine turning to God. The prophecy of Joel we referred to above underlines this very point. 'Return to me with all your heart', says the Lord through his prophet. 'Rend your hearts and not your clothing' (Joel 2.12,13). The matter is addressed with particular directness in Isaiah 58. There, the people of God ask

> Why do we fast, but you do not see?
> Why humble ourselves, but you do not notice?

> (Isaiah 58.3)

The Lord's response is swift and acerbic:

> Is such the fast that I choose,
> a day to humble oneself?
> Is it to bow down the head like a bulrush,
> and to lie in sackcloth and ashes?
> Will you call this a fast,
> a day acceptable to the Lord?
>
> Is not this the fast that I choose:
> to loose the bonds of injustice,
> to undo the thongs of the yoke,
> to let the oppressed go free,
> and to break every yoke?
> Is it not to share your bread with the hungry,
> and bring the homeless poor into your house?
>
> (Isaiah 58.5-7)

In the case of Nineveh (whose people were not God's covenant people), this lesson does seem to have got through. Not only are the inhabitants to fast, the king's edict also commands them to 'turn from their evil ways and from the violence that is in their hands' (Jonah 3.8b). Serious wrongdoing is both acknowledged and decisively eschewed. At the same time, the people are directed, emphatically, to pray: 'to cry mightily to God' (v. 8a).

God, of course, does not need us to shout in order to hear us. God's response to prayer does not depend on who makes the most noise. The merest whisper is picked up at the throne of grace. But, from a human point of view, there are times when we need to express ourselves strongly in God's direction. The nature of our condition needs to be cried out, for our soul's health. The Scriptures resonate with such cries. Just a glance at a concordance will indicate how much. The Psalms provide us with a veritable cacophony. Always they come 'out of the depths' (see Psalm130.1). These cries are raw prayer:

> I cry aloud to God . . .
> In the day of my trouble, I seek the Lord.
>
> (Psalm 77.1,2)

And there is no prayer more raw than that shouted out by Jesus on the cross. In the awful darkness, he cries out with a loud voice, 'My God, my God, why have you forsaken me?' And he dies with a scream (Mark 15.34,37). *In extremis* Jesus gives full voice to the anguish of his heart. So are we given confidence to do the same, in the time of our distress.

God of mercy,
forgive our waywardness,
and accept our change of heart.
Turn from your fierce anger
and give us time for renewal.

You who go on calling us to your ways,
strengthen our will to reform.

Comprehensive repentance (3.7-9)

The king of Nineveh and his people have received and understood the message God has proclaimed to them through Jonah. They respond with their hearts, their bodies and their lifestyle. Theirs is a comprehensive repentance. So much so that it also includes the animal population. The animals are to be at one with the city's human inhabitants. They, too, are to fast, to be clothed in sackcloth, and to cry out to the Lord (vv. 7-8). Though now, to our eyes, this picture may seem strange – perhaps amusing, perhaps exploitative – the message conveyed by the king's edict is still apposite. Human sin has consequences for the rest of God's creatures. All are caught up together in the experience of life. And, if there is to be escape from God's judgement, animals also should benefit from that salvation. In the Jonah narrative, they, quite literally, have the last word (4.11). It comes from God's lips.

Animals are important to God and valued by God – their Creator. Not one sparrow falls to the ground without the Father's awareness (Matthew 10.29). From the primal story of the Flood (Genesis 6–9) we learn that God is committed to saving the animal as well as the human creation. All are in the ark together. Despite the marring effects of human corruption and wickedness, God cannot, after all, bring himself to make a full end of that which he has so carefully and delightfully brought into being (see Genesis 1). 'God saw everything that he had made, and indeed, it was very good' (Genesis 1.31). Human sin attacks that goodness and undermines God's purposes. The dominion of humankind over the animals (Genesis 1.28) was not meant to give licence for abuse and exploitation. It was meant to be exercised after God's image and likeness: with care, respect and an acknowledgement of vital interrelatedness. If we 'lord it' over non-human creatures, so as to cause them suffering and to upset the delicate balance of nature, then we do so at our own peril. We shall have our reward. And it will not be comfortable.

Already in Jonah's story, the significance of the animal creation in God's workings has become apparent. A creature of the deep (often thought to be the instigator of chaos) has proved, in fact, to be an agent of God's salvation and a paragon of obedient response. The fish that swallows Jonah is not a solitary example of such creaturely service. Among other examples in the Bible, we might recall the ravens who obeyed the command of God to bring food to Elijah as he hid himself by the Cherith brook in a time of severe drought (1 Kings 17.1-6). Famously, too, the prophet Balaam's donkey 'saw the angel of the Lord standing in the road, with a drawn sword in his hand; so the donkey turned off the road, and went into the field' (Numbers 22.23). Balaam was not so perceptive. But the beast he ill-treated saved his life (22.33).

The poets who produced the Psalms were particularly sensitive to the place of animals in God's provision and God's affections. Here are some examples:

> The Lord is good to all,
>> and his compassion is over all that he has
>>> made . . .
> The eyes of all look to you,
>> and you give them their food in due season.
> You open your hand,
>> satisfying the desire of every living thing.
>>>> (Psalm 145.9,15-16)

> Sing to the Lord with thanksgiving . . .
>> He gives to the animals their food,
>> and to the young ravens when they cry.
>>>> (Psalm 147.7,9)

> Praise the Lord from the earth,
>> you sea monsters and all deeps . . .
> Wild animals and all cattle,
>> creeping things and flying birds!
>>>> (Psalm 148.7,10)

From the last example, we see that animals ('after their kind', as Genesis 1 puts it) have their distinctive contribution to make to that great symphony of praise that should be creation's constant response to its Creator. As James Montgomery puts it in an eighteenth-century hymn, 'And will man alone be dumb?'.[1]

The prophet Joel has no doubt that, as animals suffer the effects of disaster and human sin, so they also will enjoy God's blessing. In his words:

> Even the wild animals cry to you
> >   because the watercourses are dried up,
> and fire has devoured
> >   the pastures of the wilderness . . .
>
> Do not fear, you animals of the field,
> >   for the pastures of the wilderness are green;
> the tree bears its fruit,
> >   the fig tree and vine give their full yield.
>
> (Joel 1.20; 2.22)

This is not sentimentality. This is, first, an acute and telling awareness that all is not well with God's world. It is then a spiritual discernment that God would have it otherwise; a vision that the entire creation is intended to glorify God and thus, in a way that is fitting, know joy and peace. But God has done far more than point to a distant ideal for those who have eyes to see. He has already laid bare the heart of the matter. 'God so loved the *world* that he gave his only Son' (John 3.16). That love-offering holds out hope, and challenges us to work with God for its realization. For God's Son is the One for whom and through whom all things were created (Colossians 1.16), who upholds all things by his word of power (Hebrews 1.3) and in whom all things hold together (Colossians 1.17).

The king of Nineveh, as we encounter him in the Jonah story, has at least an inkling that, for both God and humankind, animals are of key significance. In this, as in his ready repentance, we have much to learn from him. As another psalmist puts it,

> Your righteousness is like the mighty mountains,
> your judgements are like the great deep;
> you save humans and animals alike, O Lord.
>
> (Psalm 36.6)

If we will allow it.

God of creation,
you call us to be at one with all you have made.
Forgive our misuse of creation,
our abuse of animals,
and our self-centredness.

You who feed all who look to you,
help us to care for all your creatures.

God responds (3.10)

When God saw what they did, how they turned from
their evil ways, God changed his mind about the
calamity that he had said he would bring upon them;
and he did not do it.

In issuing his decree, the king of Nineveh asks, 'Who knows? God may relent
and change his mind; he may turn from his fierce anger, so that we do not perish.'
The prophet Joel, in urging his people to return to the Lord their God, poses the
same question: 'Who knows whether he will not turn and relent?' (Joel 2.14).
The answer to the question, in both cases and in all cases, is that God alone
knows. God's actions are determined by God's sovereign prerogative. Within
the 'constraints' of God's essential nature, God does what God wills. God will
not, therefore, be swayed by any attempts (ritual or otherwise) to manipulate
divine behaviour.

In the case of the Ninevites, their radical repentance does result in God's removal
of the threat of catastrophe. As they turn to God in acknowledgement of their sin,
so God turns to them, not in condemnation but in mercy. As Jonah rightly (but
disapprovingly) perceives, mercy and grace are integral to God's very nature (4.2).
God's 'fierce anger' against sin is, in truth, a passionate expression of his love.
Love desires the very best for the beloved. Love feels and takes to heart the
damage done by sin, with its unfailing capacity to work against what is good
and to bring disorder, hurt and destruction in its wake. When the God of love
sees waste, cruelty and suffering, it is not surprising that strong reaction is stirred.
But this passion of love burns with a longing that things should be put right.
God seizes every opportunity to be gracious. In love, and in respect for human
freedom, however, God both works and waits for permission.

It is in this sense that God 'changes his mind'. God's primary purpose is that those who have given themselves over to destruction and corrupting wrongdoing should recognize their condition and find their way back to well-being. That is why God has gone to so much trouble to communicate his message to the people of Nineveh. They have only to look in God's direction to know the redeeming power of his love. Where there is humble receptivity, God's grace can have its way. As God puts it through the prophecy of Jeremiah,

> At one moment I may declare concerning a nation or a
> kingdom, that I will pluck up and break down and
> destroy it, but if that nation, concerning which I have
> spoken, turns from its evil, I will change my mind
> about the disaster that I intended to bring on it.
>
> (Jeremiah 18.7-8)

That God's desire to save is central to his character is brought home to us in Jesus. Jesus fleshes out the truth of God, both in his life and teaching and in his death and resurrection. When we look to Jesus, we see what God is like and we are drawn into God's presence. There, we most certainly find mercy and grace (see Hebrews 4.14-16). We are also challenged to the roots of our being. Exposure to divine love shows up acutely our need for forgiveness *and* amendment of life. Neither of those is without difficulty! So found many of the people who encountered Jesus during his ministry. Interestingly, it was often those who counted themselves religious who found it the hardest. They kept the rules, held to the traditions and set an example. All well and good – but not when such attitudes and practices block out the truth and the *demand* of God's love. Many of Jesus' parables put their finger on this, which is why so often they rattled those who thought they knew all about the things of God. In many ways, these folk are like latter-day Jonahs. Though the Lord tries, again and again, they will not open themselves to a message that does not fit their preconceptions. Meanwhile, those whose religious pedigree is not so impressive hear and respond much more readily. Both tendencies are still very much with us.

One parable that points this up very starkly is that of the Pharisee and the tax-collector (Luke 18.9-14). Luke informs us that Jesus 'told this parable to some who trusted in themselves that they were righteous and regarded others with contempt'. Jesus paints a vivid picture. Two men went up to the Temple to pray, one a Pharisee, the other a tax-collector; one a religious leader, punctilious in his observance, the other a despised and far from observant collaborator with the Roman occupying power and liner of his own pockets. The Pharisee's style of prayer was to stand by himself (thus reducing the risk of spiritual contamination) and then to remind God what an exemplary person was coming before him: 'God, I thank you that I am not like other people: thieves, rogues, adulterers, or even like this tax-collector. I fast twice a week; I give a tenth of all my income.' By contrast, the maligned tax-collector stands 'far off', hanging his head and praying, 'God, be merciful to me, a sinner'. 'I tell you,' says Jesus, 'this man went down to his home justified rather than the other.'

Jesus no doubt caricatures to press home his point. But his characters are still recognizable. Perhaps there is something of both in most of us. Jonah would certainly applaud the Pharisee. The people of Nineveh take the approach of the tax-collector. They would surely have warmed to Jesus' nutshell summary of his mission: 'The Son of Man came to seek out and save the lost' (Luke 19.10). He does this in many and various ways, as the four Gospel accounts show us. In the end, it becomes too much for the official guardians of religion. Despite all God's best efforts, they cannot see that they, too, are lost and in need of mercy. Jesus is seen as a threat to the health of God's people – someone, therefore, to be got rid of. Yet even this, God, painfully, works together for good. What happened on Calvary becomes the greatest act of redemption ever. God's love will not be thwarted, even when it is being crucified. As Paul put it in an incomparable poetic passage:

> [Love] bears all things, believes all things, hopes all
> things, endures all things.
> Love never ends.

> (1 Corinthians 13.7-8)

Jonah was encouraged to struggle with this. So are we.

God of surprises,
thank you for giving us time,
thank you for giving us hope.
Accept our change of heart
and help us hold on to our resolve.

You who go on calling us to yourself,
strengthen our will to return.

God's mercy for all (overview of Jonah 3)

This chapter leaves us in no doubt that God's mercy is comprehensive in its scope. God's compassion is, indeed, over all his works (Psalm 145.9). God's urgent desire is to save, to bring out the best, to express his all-embracing love for all creation. But it is also true that love and mercy have to be accepted if they are to work their work. They cannot be forced. The freedom of choice given to humankind is real. We are free to turn our backs on God. We are free to close our eyes to the truth of our condition. We are free to ignore our crying need of God's grace. For all that, God will not cease, by all manner of means, to try to get through to us.

So Jonah discovered. Having run away, God's outstretched hand brought him back. He is saved from the consequences of his rebellion and, for a second time, given his missionary marching orders. 'Failure' is a word that does not seem to figure very significantly in God's vocabulary. What might be thus defined is presented by God as an opportunity to learn the lessons of love. Love transforms everything – even the worst of things. The cross is the supreme sign of that. In the case of Jonah, the lessons to be learned from his failure should have been crystal clear. God has not punished him for his sin. Rather, God has delivered him. Might that not be relevant to the way God chooses to behave towards other recalcitrant souls? But, as will soon become apparent, Jonah finds it very difficult to extrapolate from his own experience. In relation to Jonah, God's task is not an easy one.

The Ninevites and their king prove much more responsive. The message proclaimed through Jonah clearly strikes fear into their hearts. But it is not fear that predominates. Their fear unlocks genuine repentance. It shows them up for what they are, and they determine to do something about it. God's mercy thus finds an open channel. This foreign city, in a nation that is hardly friendly towards God's covenant people, sets an example of faith. It is also revealed as just as much the object of God's care as the prophet God has sent to them. This is a crucial feature of the overall message of Jonah's story. It was the task of God's chosen ones, privileged with God's special attention, to share this experience with God's wider world, to be 'a light to the nations, that my salvation may reach to the ends of the earth', as Isaiah puts it (Isaiah 49.6). The temptation, however, was always towards being exclusive and, therefore, judgemental. If God had chosen them as his special possession, then God must be theirs, and no one else's, to possess. Those outside the boundaries could not, surely, be worthy of God's mercy. Such a tendency (like sin) 'lurks at the door' of any community committed to God (see Genesis 4.7). God's servants, however, are bidden to proceed with all boldness through the door, breaking out, in all kinds of senses, to participate in the (sometimes surprising) mission of God. There are many Ninevehs to engage with, for God's sake. That cannot be done from behind closed doors (see John 20.19-23).

Jonah (who stands for so many across the centuries) needs to learn that God's loving attention can never be confined to a particular people or territory. It is exercised always and everywhere, as well as in each particular case. As the psalmist declared, 'The earth is the Lord's and all that is in it' (Psalm 24.1). The 'all' most certainly includes God's animal creation. Non-human living beings matter to God. They should also matter to us. In their own way, the animals of Nineveh, along with the city's human inhabitants, experienced God's ministry of mercy. That is entirely fitting for a God who is the source of all that exists and who, at all times and in all places, takes responsibility for his creation.

In rightly perceiving God's close concern with the animal world, the biblical writers feel free to use animal imagery to try to communicate God's character and ways. In essence, of course, God defies (and is greater than) all our description. Any picture language we turn to should not be taken literally. Yet God has given us the capacity to know him in love, and longs for us to do so. One aid to such knowing is to observe the world around us – the world God so lovingly and imaginatively brought into being. 'The heavens are telling the glory of God' (Psalm 19.1). So are the animals, if we take the trouble to look out for their signals. As we read the Scriptures, it is well worth keeping an eye out for 'connections' of this kind picked up by our forebears. Birds, for example, are found to be suggestive in this respect, not least the eagle, speaking of God's strength, freedom and care. All three characteristics come together in a passage to be found at Deuteronomy 32.11-12:

> As an eagle stirs up its nest,
>   and hovers over its young;
> as it spreads its wings, takes them up,
>   and bears them aloft on its pinions,
> the Lord alone guided [Israel].

A rather more domestic and down-to-earth fowl is chosen by Jesus to convey his longing to bless and protect Jerusalem: 'How often have I desired to gather your children together as a hen gathers her brood under her wing, and you were not willing!' (Luke 13.34).

Earth-bound creatures also feature significantly in the biblical record as metaphors and similes for the working of God. Some express the overwhelming power of God, and the threat posed by his fierce passion. So with the bear, the lion and the leopard. Hosea's usage is particularly striking (and frightening):

> So I will become like a lion to them,
>   like a leopard I will lurk beside the way.
> I will fall upon them like a bear robbed of her cubs,
>   and will tear open the covering of their heart;
> there I will devour them like a lion,
>   as a wild animal would mangle them.
>
> (Hosea 13.7-8; see also Lamentations 3.10)

That is truly a fearsome image of judgement. Yet it must be seen in the wider context of Hosea's prophecy. The strong language comes from strong feelings – feelings of faithful love betrayed. They need to be expressed and heard, so that the enormity of the betrayal may be exposed and taken to heart. But from behind this ferocious imagery comes another word – word of a love that, though desperately hurt, cannot bring itself to reciprocate the experience. 'How can I give you up, Ephraim? . . . I will not execute my fierce anger . . . I will not again destroy' (Hosea 11.8,9).

That latter prophecy is emphatically fulfilled in the coming of Jesus. A very different animal metaphor has to be employed to convey something of the meaning and character of his mission of love. As John the Baptist puts it in John's Gospel: 'Here is the Lamb of God who takes away the sin of the world!' (John 1.29). Here is an image of total and (in his case) willing vulnerability. Here is a love-offering beyond *all* compare.

God of compassion,
the earth is yours and all that is in it,
help us to play our full part in caring for it.

Guidelines for groups (3)

Sharing together (30 mins)

1. Briefly update each other on the outcome of actions agreed at the last meeting.

2. Ask everyone to give their initial impressions from reading Jonah 3 and the study material. If you can, share one thing you gained and one question you bring.

3. Share any experiences you've had of speaking out against what you felt to be wrong. How did it affect you?

Studying together (40 mins)

1. How often do we say 'no' to a request when we know in our hearts we should comply? Are we brave or honest enough to reconsider? How do we go about witnessing to what we believe God wants of his people – including us?

2. The second time round, Jonah acts on God's prompting. In the midst of our busy-ness, are we alert enough to hear God's word for us? As a church, are we confident enough to proclaim God's message – especially when it is unpalatable to many?

3. What does Jonah 3 have to teach us about God's care for people and animals?

4. Over the last few years, national and international events have reached deep into people's lives: terrorist attacks, especially 9/11, the death of royalty, the threats and the reality of war. Can we learn anything from Nineveh?

5. Where else in Scripture might you find God changing his mind? Does it ring true?

Taking action together (10 mins)

1. How could our church communities fulfil their prophetic calling? Think of ways to challenge society's sinfulness with a call to repentance and the message of God's love.

2. Suggest ways in which we can show greater respect and care for God's non-human creation.

Prayer together (20 mins)

1. First set the scene to allow the group to change gear. You may want to have a two-minute break, rearrange the chairs, or set up a visual focus for prayer such as an icon or candles.

2. Begin with a prayer asking for the Lord of mercy and understanding to be present with you. Follow this with a time of quiet: use either the silence or a piece of quiet music to allow hearts and minds to be still.

3. The leader should choose two or three key passages from Jonah 3, reading them slowly, leaving plenty of space between the chosen sections.

4. After you have pictured the scenes in your mind, imagine yourself as part of the population of Nineveh. Would you want to support the king? What would you want to say to God? What sort of reply would you expect?

5. End with silence, music or a quiet song and a final prayer.

6. There may be things members want to note down in a journal or share with others. Go on reflecting on the passage, on your meditation, and on encountering the God of Jesus Christ through the coming week.

Chapter 4

Exploring Anger – Jonah 4

An angry prophet (4.1-3)

> But this was very displeasing to Jonah, and he became
> angry. He prayed to the Lord and said, 'O Lord! Is not
> this what I said while I was still in my own country?
> That is why I fled to Tarshish at the beginning; for I
> knew that you are a gracious God and merciful, slow
> to anger, and abounding in steadfast love, and ready
> to relent from punishing. And now, O Lord, please
> take my life from me, for it is better for me to die
> than to live.'

It has to be said that, from beginning to end of his adventure, Jonah does not
come out well. In this closing episode, he blatantly shows his true colours. They
are not very attractive. But that is very much the narrator's intention: to paint
the folly of Jonah's attitude so vividly that those who see it will be challenged to
confront the stupidity of their own prejudice. Jonah's story is meant to be tough
spiritual education, not just light entertainment. Like Jesus the teacher, however,
this communicator knows that more may well be achieved through an engaging
tale than through a heavy lecture.

So the repugnant reality of narrow-minded judgementalism is clearly set before us
in the person of Jonah. The pathetic weakness of its 'arguments' is (almost
brutally) exposed. Jonah is ruthlessly shown up for the mean, petty and petulant
person he is. Yet he remains God's prophet. Like everyone who looks at this
fascinating portrayal, we have to ask where we might find ourselves in this
picture. In what sense might it, in fact, be a mirror, reflecting back attitudes,
perhaps barely acknowledged, in the thoughts of our hearts?

When Jonah eventually embarked on his mission, he did not know for certain
what God might do as a result of his preaching. Originally, God had told him to
'cry out' against Nineveh 'for their wickedness has come up before me' (1.2). The
message Jonah has been given to proclaim, 'Forty days more, and Nineveh shall
be overthrown' (3.4), might have led him to expect (and hope for) a destructive
outcome. Yet his own experience of God's saving mercy thus far should have told

him otherwise; as, indeed, should the existing theological knowledge that becomes apparent in his angry outburst against God (4.2). But when God spares the city, Jonah is furious. The strong language used in verse 1 to describe his reaction leaves us in no doubt that Jonah is beside himself with rage. His anger is born not out of passionate concern but of blind prejudice. And it is directed against God.

Jonah is mightily displeased that God should have saved an unfriendly and corrupt foreign power instead of giving them their just deserts. God has not come up to Jonah's standard of judgement. Indeed, we get the distinct impression that Jonah does not really like God very much! Fortunately, that antipathy does not seem to be mutual. At this stage, however, Jonah does at least remember to pray. He now shares his feelings with the Lord, thus allowing God to pursue an instructive, if challenging, dialogue. In the biblical record, this comes across as one of God's favoured methods of encouraging learning and change. With such a sparring partner as Jonah, God's task is far from easy. But God, too, it seems, relishes a challenge.

It now becomes clear, by Jonah's own admission, why he ran away from God's commission in the first place. It was not because he was afraid or felt inadequate, but because he strongly disapproved of what he sensed God was asking and planning. It transpires that Jonah knew God well enough to suspect that his calling was not the satisfying (if perhaps dangerous) proclamation of inevitable doom. It carried the distinct possibility that God would not destroy but save. The possibility turns into actuality. Jonah's worst suspicions are confirmed. He therefore rounds on God – but in such a way that his own hardness of heart is laid bare.

Jonah appears to regard the divine qualities of grace, mercy and steadfast love as traits to be deplored rather than gifts to be thankfully affirmed and received. Yet, as he must have known, these expressions of God's character were at the heart of God's covenant relationship with his people. On Mount Sinai

> the Lord passed before [Moses], and proclaimed,
> 'The Lord, the Lord,
> a God merciful and gracious,
> slow to anger,
> and abounding in steadfast love and faithfulness.'
> (Exodus 34.6; see also Psalms 86.15; 103.8; 145.8; Joel 2.13)

Knowing that God's loving anger, though slow to be aroused, is quickly translated into mercy, Jonah could see what might be coming. And he did not like it. Steadfast love and relenting from punishment were fine for God's chosen people (and, of course, Jonah), but they were surely not appropriate for enemies and oppressors. It is no accident that Jonah refers to 'my own country' (v. 2) in this regard. He cannot bear the thought (though he recognizes its likelihood) that God's mercy might be more than an exclusive property for the specially favoured. As King Solomon perceived in a different context, 'Even heaven and the highest heaven cannot contain you, much less this house that I have built!' (1 Kings 8.27). God will not be trapped in any particular set of expectations or desires.

In his response to God's generosity, Jonah is not unlike the elder brother in the parable of the Prodigal Son (see Luke 15.25-32). The returning prodigal's brother becomes angry when he hears what a song and dance his father is making over a good-for-nothing wastrel. 'He doesn't deserve it' is the ill-tempered complaint, 'And what about *me*?' His whining self-centredness echoes that of Jonah. Both characters need their eyes and their hearts opened to a lavishly loving God – a God who, if they could only see it, showers blessings on them also. It is not a case of 'either/or' but of 'both/and'. In truth, it is God who is prodigal – with his grace (see John 1.16).

Jonah, however, is determined to apply the wet blanket. His sulkiness descends into a death wish. He asks God to take his life – that same God who has just gone to such enormous trouble to save it. God ignores that request. He won't be manipulated by Jonah's professed suicidal condition (was he trying to make God feel guilty?). There is an important lesson now to be delivered.

God of contradiction,
why do you change your mind?
Just when we think we know your ways
you seem to act out of character.

Teach us your ways,
that we may live out your truth.

A questioning God (4.4-5)

> And the Lord said, 'Is it right for you to be angry?'
> Then Jonah went out of the city and sat down east of
> the city, and made a booth for himself there. He sat
> under it in the shade, waiting to see what would
> become of the city.

As we noted earlier (see Chapter 1), the God of the Scriptures is a God of sharp and pertinent questions. At the time of the storm at sea, God's questions had come through unwitting (and foreign) sailors. Now God himself puts Jonah on the spot. With one devastating and repeated question, God exposes the heart of the matter: 'Is it right for you to be angry?' (4.4,9).

We are reminded, perhaps, of another dramatic encounter in which the Lord questions the rightness of someone's anger – that of Cain (Genesis 4.1-16). In this foundational story, Cain is full of wrath because God has acted in a way he neither understands nor appreciates. God has favoured someone else (his brother, Abel). God has not taken into account Cain's own wishes and feelings. God is being decidedly unfair. 'So Cain was very angry and his countenance fell. The Lord said to Cain, 'Why are you angry, and why has your countenance fallen? If you do well, will you not be accepted? And if you do not do well, sin is lurking at the door; its desire is for you, but you must master it.' Cain does not master it. He responds to God's probing by turning murderously on his brother. Jonah responds by turning a death wish on himself. Yet tragedy is stayed because he has turned first to the Lord.

Self-centred and jealous anger, it seems, is a deep-rooted and persistent flaw in the human character. It has so often led to heartbreak and bloodshed. Anger itself is a deeply ambivalent emotion. Its energy can achieve much that is good. It can also bring destruction. A great deal depends on where the anger is rooted and how it is given expression. If it is to be properly incarnated and purified, it belongs in the love of God. Jonah certainly 'did right' to offload his anger on to God. God knows what to do with it. God can take it – and work to redeem it. We see that supremely on Calvary. On the cross, God's Word made flesh feels the full impact of the sin of the world, destructive anger very much included. Out of that awful and bitter experience comes forgiveness beyond measure. God does not 'fight back', except with the instruments of absolute love and resurrection life.

Like Jonah, then, we should first and foremost take our anger to God in prayer. If we spit it out in that context, it may be that God can use it for healing. Such prayer may also be 'the stay of our hand' in relation to inappropriate action. God can use it, too, to deepen our awareness and widen our understanding, so that we discern more about ourselves and the situation that is inflaming us. For many, it may indeed be necessary to vent their feelings in the safety of God's presence before they can begin to take to heart the gospel imperative to love enemies and forgive those who cause hurt. A soul bursting with the venom of vengeance has no capacity for the medicine of love.

The psalmists certainly had no reticence in frankly sharing their negativity with God. Sometimes (by implication, rather like Jonah) they clamour for God to exercise divine anger on those who oppose them:

> Pour out your indignation upon them,
>   and let your burning anger overtake them.
>
> (Psalm 69.24)

> Pour out your anger on the nations
>   that do not know you,
> and on the kingdoms
>   that do not call upon your name.
>
> (Psalm 79.6)

Jonah would surely say 'Amen' to both prayers! When we find ourselves doing so, however, we need to hear a quiet yet insistent command coming back in our direction: 'Put away from you all bitterness and wrath and anger . . .' (Ephesians 4.31). God knows that is no easy thing to do. Our prayer will most probably need to include ongoing objections and admissions of failure. But honest openness to God can at least make a difference to the set of our wills. And in sharing our hurt, it can help to remember that we do so with a wounded God. God, indeed, *knows*.

Is Jonah right to be angry? The answer to that has to be 'no' – though Jonah is left to work that out for himself. Is it ever right to be angry? That can be answered in the affirmative. Though 'slow to anger', God is most certainly familiar with the emotion, if the biblical record is anything to go by. What sparks his wrath is behaviour such as injustice, unrighteousness, gross failure of love, betrayal, exploitation of the poor and the alien, selfish greed and the misuse of power – in other words, abuse of community and personal relationships in such a way as to bring suffering and unhealthy disorder. Or, even more succinctly, rejection of

God's love and blessing. That grieves God mightily. So much potential for good is being thrown away. Things must be put right.

When we 'hunger and thirst for righteousness' (Matthew 5.6) we may well touch something of God's passion. There are many things in this world (too many) that should rightly make us angry. What we do with that anger still matters, critically. As the writer of Ephesians put it: 'Be angry but do not sin' (Ephesians 4.26). There must be ways of confronting wrong that do not add to its tally. There was an occasion in the ministry of Jesus when the disciples James and John wanted to command fire to come down from heaven and consume a Samaritan village that would not receive Jesus. But Jesus 'turned and rebuked them' (Luke 9.51-55). In standing boldly for God's righteousness, we have constant need of God's grace and guidance. If we are to participate in God's passionate mission to grow the values of his kingdom, then prayer must again be of the essence. The temptation to self-righteousness is ever real.

Jonah is not just self-righteous but also self-pitying. He clearly finds it difficult to cope with God's direct and critical question. His response is to get out of Nineveh, yet again trying to distance himself from 'the problem'. This time, however, he stays close enough to see what will happen. Perhaps even at this stage, the Lord will come to his senses and destroy the wicked. Was that not the message with which he had been entrusted? And was not God bound to fulfil his word? Jonah must have felt very frustrated in his conviction that he knew better than God.

God of questions,
why do you press your case?
What can we do
but to wait on your responses?

Teach us your ways,
that we may live out your love.

An educational experience (4.6-11)

The Lord God appointed a bush, and made it come
up over Jonah, to give shade over his head, to save him
from his discomfort; so Jonah was very happy about
the bush. But when dawn came up the next day, God
appointed a worm that attacked the bush, so that it

withered. When the sun rose, God prepared a sultry
east wind, and the sun beat down on the head of
Jonah so that he was faint and asked that he might
die. He said, 'It is better for me to die than to live.'
But God said to Jonah, 'Is it right for you to be angry
about the bush?' And he said, 'Yes, angry enough to
die.' Then the Lord said, 'You are concerned about the
bush, for which you did not labour and which you did
not grow; it came into being in a night and perished in
a night. And should I not be concerned about Nineveh,
that great city, in which there are more than a hundred
and twenty thousand persons who do not know their
right hand from their left, and also many animals?'

What Jonah has proclaimed with a bad grace, God's grace has taken hold of
for good. The recipients of Jonah's preaching have clearly seen its implications
much more effectively than the preacher. Now, God makes a concerted attempt
to penetrate the prejudice of his prophet. The divine determination to educate as
well as save comes to the fore.

The God of the Scriptures is most certainly a teacher. Again and again, he tries
all manner of means to get his message through, to open up understanding, to
enable his beloved and exasperating human creation to learn the lessons of
righteous love. It is not surprising, then, that when God comes among us in Jesus,
teaching forms a very significant part of his ministry. It is teaching that makes a
real impact. It engages the attention, and frequently issues sharp challenge. It
makes much use of vivid illustrations from everyday life – but its message is by
no means simple and straightforward. It often leaves even the closest disciples of
Jesus struggling for understanding. Deliberately so. We have to work out and
explore God's meaning for ourselves. Only in this way will the learning truly
become part of us and bear fruit in our behaviour. That is why, not infrequently,
God's 'teaching units' include questions (not least at the beginning and/or the end).

So it is with the 'lesson' experienced by Jonah. It takes the form of a dialogue and
it ends with a question. It also (yet again) uses non-human creation as a teaching
aid. God 'appoints' (the same verb is used earlier of the fish) a plant and a worm
as teaching assistants.

First, God uses the natural world to protect his angry, sullen servant from the
searing heat. Jonah is both comforted and pleased. Then God employs one of his

creatures to destroy that which had brought protection. Jonah is consumed with displeasure. How could God treat his servant thus? Overwhelmed by the wind and the sun (also about the Lord's business) and feeling within himself a burning indignation, Jonah insists that he is right to be angry about the demise of the plant – so angry he could die. He uses the same phrase he had thrown at God a little earlier: 'It is better for me to die than to live' (v. 8, see also v. 3). Jonah's anger against God has clearly not been abated. Neither has his attempt to manipulate God into a form of behaviour more to his own liking. It really is all very childish. It is also very recognizable human behaviour, whether directed against God or more earthly subjects.

Nonetheless, all unwittingly, Jonah has played into God's hands. The lesson is about to be brought home. Purely out of immediate self-interest, Jonah is 'concerned' about a short-lived plant that he had no part in producing. How much more should God be 'concerned' about the many inhabitants of Nineveh, animal as well as human. They are all of God's making and God has their interests at heart. Should not God do all in his power to save them from disaster? The human population was lost in wickedness, not knowing 'their right hand from their left', that is, not knowing the difference between right and wrong. That is why Jonah was sent to them; to open their eyes to the truth. Should not Jonah be rejoicing at their repentance and deliverance, rather than complaining against God?

We are not told how Jonah responded to his lesson. Instead, we are left to make our own response to the fundamental issues Jonah's story has raised.

God of mystery,
why do you lead us on?
We see you as protector
yet feel a contrariness of concern.

Teach us your ways,
that we may live out your life.

Not just a funny story (overview of Jonah 4)

It would be easy just to laugh at Jonah, gone off in a sulk because God would not do what he wanted. He does indeed cut an amusing as well as a pathetic figure. As we smile at him, however, we would do well to consider that we may, in fact, be laughing at ourselves. The narrator of Jonah's story is not simply wanting to make its readers laugh. The humour of the tale is a route to a deeper understanding and clearer vision. It is designed to show up the shortcomings in the readers' own attitudes and behaviour. In this regard, the story of Jonah is akin to many of the parables of Jesus.

The God we encounter in Jonah most certainly has much to teach us. We can hardly escape the conclusion that God is, indeed, an educator, a committed communicator. The lesson delivered to Jonah outside Nineveh underlines that (fortunately) God does not give up on slow learners or persistent offenders. In the cause of opening the heart and mind of Jonah to the truth, God exploits a whole range of methods, not least dialogue, astute questioning, visual aids and the encouraging of reflection upon experience. This God cares enough to persevere – and to take risks. On the risk scale, the uncooperative Jonah must score quite highly.

But God chose Jonah and worked with him as he was. From the Scriptures more generally, it seems that God consistently calls into particular service those who appear less than ideal candidates. In Jonah's case, it is stubborn bigotry rather than any sense of personal unworthiness that makes him pull back from God's will. It is interesting to note that, though during the course of the story all the characters are delivered from serious threat, only the pagan sailors and the wicked Ninevites are clearly converted. Whether Jonah 'repents' remains an open question at the end of the narrative. He had finally done God's bidding. Did he also come to see the light of God's loving wisdom? Was he able not only to 'forgive' God but also to rejoice in God's gracious mercy? Or did he continue to nurse his self-centred anger? The choice was his. Just as the choice is ours.

It is a choice that matters. For the God of Jonah is not just a dedicated and imaginative teacher, who specializes in difficult cases. This deity is sovereign Lord of all. From beginning to end of Jonah's story, God displays his authority over all creation. In the opening episode, the wild forces of chaos are at God's bidding. In the closing scene, rather humbler manifestations of God's creativity play their part in God's purposes. The lowly plant and worm carry their messages from the Almighty. They signal that, in the exercise of power, God is neither cruel nor capricious. Though Jonah's immediate experience might make it feel to be otherwise, God's purpose is entirely positive – to make it clear that God's compassion is indeed over all he has made. It is the universal dimension of God's longing that Jonah cannot stomach. His physical discomfort in the oppressive heat is but a palpable sign of a soul deeply troubled. Surely God should wreak vengeance upon sinners who are his people's enemies. Such attitudes are not, of course, confined to Jonah. And when deep suffering has been caused, they are profoundly understandable. God's searching forgiveness, however, is open to all – and all are invited to turn and receive it.

It is clear that, if Jonah were God, grace, mercy and steadfast love would be in much shorter supply than punishment (see 4.2). Part of Jonah's anger is that he has been denied the satisfaction of seeing his perceived 'enemies' perish. That would have made him feel much better. Yet the God who dialogues with Jonah speaks his message with even more challenging directness in Jesus:

> You have heard that it was said, 'You shall love
> your neighbour and hate your enemy.' But I say
> to you, Love your enemies and pray for those who
> persecute you, so that you may be children of your
> Father in heaven; for he makes his sun rise on the
> evil and on the good, and sends rain on the righteous
> and the unrighteous.'
>
> (Matthew 5.43-45; see also Romans 12.14-21).

God's gracious provision is for everyone. And love and prayer are essential weapons in the battle against evil and hatred. Only so are vicious circles penetrated. Only so is true redemption won. But such love and prayer do not often come naturally. They are born of a struggle that has the cross of Christ at its heart.

It is the God of Jesus Christ who is judge of all (Hebrews 12.23). We should not presume to make his judgements for him. And it is always salutary to remember that judgement begins 'with the household of God' (1 Peter 4.17). Like Jonah, we do not always find it easy to look to ourselves in this respect. It is far more attractive to condemn others than to face up to our own shortcomings.

God of challenge,
why do we miss the point?
How can we learn to judge
with your judgement of love?

Teach us your ways,
to love enemies as ourselves.

The message of Jonah

The story of Jonah is a story well told. The fact that it is tightly narrated only serves to heighten its dramatic effect. We are given very little contextual detail. There is no padding out of the narrative. Yet the author's powers of description quickly engage us with the heart of the matter. Jonah's rebellious flight and the crisis of the storm, for example, have all the more impact on us because they come suddenly, out of the blue. And we soon realize that we are being introduced to something more than just an interesting tale. This 'adventure story' comes uncomfortably close to home, with its laying bare of attitudes, reactions and fundamental questions.

It is all the more effective for having a distinct edge of comedy. As we have noted, the dimension of humour helps us to see more clearly. In chuckling at Jonah, we are perhaps readier to perceive something of ourselves in him and his situation. Truth can be easier to deal with when expressed through the wry laughter of recognition.

This narrator is gentle but razor sharp. Humour there may be, but it is in the service of a serious message. This is no send-up. Nor is Jonah ridiculed. Though his weaknesses are made all too apparent, they are woven into God's purposes of redemption. This is a crucial strand in the whole narrative. Failure and shortcomings do not result in expulsion from God's presence or God's favour. Far from it. Contrary to popular trends in our modern society, the one who performs abysmally is not 'voted out' by God. Jonah, the stubborn coward, becomes an example of God's providence and a partner in God's ministry. The 'weakest link' is essential to God's chain of grace.

Through the drama of Jonah, a good many key issues are opened up. They all revolve round the character and working of God. Two theological words are of primary significance in this regard: sovereignty and providence.

The narrator of Jonah's story clearly wants us to understand (and accept) that God is Lord of all. God's sovereign power and concern are universal in their reach and comprehensive in their scope. Nothing and no one lie outside God's sphere of activity, whether it be the inhabitants of sinful Nineveh, a disobedient prophet, pagan mariners, foreign parts, the natural elements or non-human creation. In relation to all of them, God is the controlling force. But this is no divine tyranny – God's sovereignty is characterized by providential love.

When God 'made the sea and the dry land' (Jonah 1.9), he looked on everything that he had made, 'and indeed, it was very good' (Genesis 1.31). God's continued working in and with his creation is also suffused and motivated by goodness – the goodness that is the fruit of God's perfect love. One of the profoundest insights into this truth comes from the fourteenth-century English mystic, Julian of

Norwich. She recounts how, in a situation of personal suffering, God showed her spiritually 'a little thing, the size of a hazelnut, on the palm of my hand, round like a ball. I looked at it thoughtfully and wondered, "What is this?" And the answer came, "It is all that is made." I marvelled that it continued to exist and did not suddenly disintegrate; it was so small. And again my mind supplied the answer, "It exists, both now and for ever, because God loves it." In short, everything owes its existence to the love of God'.[1]

The sovereignty of God is that power of love. Such was the lesson Jonah (and not only he) needed to learn. Even in the wild turbulence, God has everyone's good at heart, including the one who has badly let him down.

All this should be a source of great encouragement. It also leaves us grappling with some acutely painful questions. Such questions begin to expose some of the deeper chasms in our understanding. We are all too well aware of the dark and destructive side of both the natural elements and human nature. How can these things be, if all is under the goodly rule of God? Is God's power not absolute? Does God's goodness have limits? If this is a God who does desire the best, why does he not act to prevent flood, mayhem and murder – to name but a few tragic scenarios? Where are sovereignty and providence in the killing of innocents?

The writer of the Book of Jonah does not, of course, set out to answer these fundamental questions. By his approach to Jonah's story, however, he does most certainly raise them if only by implication and provocation. They are particularly searing when, like the sailors, we ourselves are in the midst of crisis. Again, like them, we can pray and hurl questions at a God who seems either to be hurling the storm or responding to it with a deafening silence. Job also followed this course. His erstwhile 'friends' try to deflect him, persistently arguing that he should accept that his suffering must be a consequence of his sin and that God knows best. With even greater persistence, Job refuses to let God off the hook so lightly. Eventually, he breaks through to a personal experience of God that is beyond words and explanations:

> I had heard of you by the hearing of the ear,
> but now my eye sees you.
>
> (Job 42.5)

The seventeenth-century poet, George Herbert, in one of his struggles with God, came through to a similar conclusion:

> But as I rav'd and grew more fierce and wilde
> At every word,
> Me thoughts I heard one calling, *Child:*
> And I reply'd, *My Lord.*[2]

Both Job and George Herbert, like so many others, discovered, through their raw questioning, the sovereignty of God's love. It is love that will never give up. It is love that, in Jesus, has experienced the heart of darkness. It is love that, in William Blake's words, 'builds a heaven in hell's despair'.[3] Such love pursues Jonah across the sea. It finds expression in many surprising ways. It is neither soft nor unhealthily indulgent. It labours to reach where we are, to be with us there and to bring us through. It even forgives our 'enemies'. As with Jonah, that can sometimes be the hardest thing to take. Both as individuals and societies, we all have our equivalent of the Ninevites.

This love can, indeed, be called providential. It provides for us in any and every circumstance. It works tirelessly to bring out the best. But God's providence is not the same as predestination or determinism. We are not God's puppets, but God's beloved creation. We have free will. The pressure of God's love may be well nigh irresistible, in the long run at least, but resistance is most certainly possible. Many have proved it so. In the dispensation of God, love and freedom are inseparably intertwined.

Jonah could have turned his back on God's advances. The consequences would have been serious – both for Jonah and for all those drawn within the ambit of his disobedience. Sin, whether individual or corporate, always has knock-on effects. One way and another, it brings pain and strain in its wake. And always, it is the mission of God to redeem; to open eyes, hearts and wills to the life that is life indeed. If we stand out against God's redeeming grace, that can only be to our great detriment, as well as that of others. It is holy love that pursues us, even as it pursued Jonah and challenged the Ninevites.

We leave Jonah, consumed with anger and prejudice, and faced with God's searching questions. Where does that leave us?

> God of sovereign providence,
> why do we still miss the point?
> Meet us in our raving
> and probe our prejudice.

Teach us your ways,
that we may see with your eyes.

The sign of Jonah

According to the Gospel traditions, Jesus pointed to the story of Jonah as an important sign of the nature of his own vocation and ministry. So, when some of the scribes and Pharisees demanded that Jesus produce a sign to authenticate his bold preaching, he responded like this:

> An evil and adulterous generation asks for a sign,
> but no sign will be given to it except the sign of the
> prophet Jonah. For just as Jonah was three days and
> three nights in the belly of the sea monster, so for three
> days and three nights the Son of Man will be in the
> heart of the earth. The people of Nineveh will rise up
> at the judgement with this generation and condemn it,
> because they repented at the proclamation of Jonah,
> and see, something greater than Jonah is here!
>
> (Matthew 12.39-41)

A little later, Jesus gives the same message in a nutshell to Pharisees still clamouring for 'a sign from heaven' (Matthew 16.1,4). The evangelist Luke also records this pointing to the example of Jonah (Luke 11.29-32).

Jesus had come with a message of grace and mercy from God. If that message was to be fully received and enjoyed, then there would need to be repentance – a turning towards God that would enable people to perceive God's presence and know the depth of God's love. The 'kingdom of God' – that divine sovereignty that is the power of pure love – could only be realized and experienced by willing acceptance of God's gracious invitation. But many found all this very difficult to believe. The official religious leaders, particularly, were seriously challenged by Jesus and his preaching and ministry. It was not authorized. Jesus had no formal qualification or official permission to set himself up in this way. He was constantly (as the leaders saw it) undermining their authority and teaching. He did not stick to the detailed rules and rigid definitions that they regarded as essential to the carrying out and communication of God's will. Jesus looked with favour on those who did not really 'belong' – those who, for one reason or another, were regarded as being on the very edge of acceptability. Indeed, he had the temerity to claim that God's merciful care extended beyond the 'chosen people' to the Gentiles. Neither was he very much the diplomat in getting his message across. His clashes with the religious powers that be were sometimes very fierce indeed. In the instance we have quoted, Jesus refers to those around him as 'an evil and adulterous generation'. This was not restrained language!

It was, however, prophetic language. The word 'adulterous', for example, is not so much a comment on people's morals as a graphic portrayal of the people's unfaithfulness to God. Old Testament prophets had already made effective use of this image (see, for example, Jeremiah 3.8; Ezekiel 23.27; Hosea 2.2-10).

Jesus makes it very clear that the people of Nineveh (outsiders and enemies of God's people) have shown a more faithful response to God through the preaching of Jonah than those confronted with the preaching of Jesus. Yet Jesus is far greater than Jonah, the reluctant prophet. The people of Nineveh repented, and, by their behaviour, bore fruit worthy of repentance (Matthew 3.8). The people who clashed with Jesus showed no evidence that they had taken his message on board. Quite the contrary. They failed to perceive that the most effective sign of God's presence and authority was standing among them in the person of Jesus. Jesus does not match up to their expectations, and he carries a challenge that is far too disturbing.

Like Jonah (though very much more willingly), Jesus is calling for a change of heart. Like Jonah, also, Jesus will be entombed and delivered – but that will not be because of his own sin but the sin of others. Jonah's deliverance from the belly of the fish is but a dim prefiguring of God's greatest act of salvation in the death and resurrection of Jesus. One far greater than Jonah is pointing to no less than 'Emmanuel' – God with us.

When all is said and done, therefore, let Jonah point us to Jesus.

God with us,
why do we still not understand?
Why do we not recognize your coming?

Teach us your ways,
and point us to Jesus.

Guidelines for groups (4)

Sharing together (30 mins)

1. Briefly update each other on the outcome of actions agreed at the last meeting.

2. Invite all to give their initial impressions from reading Jonah 4 and the study material. If you can, share one thing you gained and one question you bring.

3. If appropriate, talk together about times when you have argued (or felt like arguing) with God.

4. Have you ever felt resentful about God's generosity to others?

Studying together (40 mins)

1. 'Is it right for you to be angry?' How might we respond to this repeated question? What makes you angry?

2. How often do we long to see the downfall of people who, in our view, shouldn't be taken seriously by God? How can we learn to rejoice when they turn back to God?

3. What might the Book of Jonah teach us about relationships between humans and animals?

4. Of the many questions posed in the text, which have struck home for you?

5. How does this passage express the depth of God's concern for creation?

Taking action together (10 mins)

1. How are you going to take forward the implications of Jonah for the mission of your church community?

2. How are you going to take forward in your personal discipleship what you have learned from Jonah?

Prayer together (20 mins)

1. First, set the scene to allow the group to change gear. You may want to have a two-minute break, rearrange the chairs, or set up a visual focus for prayer such as an icon or candles.

2. Begin with a prayer asking for the Lord of graciousness and mercy to be present with you. Follow this with a time of quiet: use either the silence or a piece of quiet music to allow hearts and minds to be still.

3. The leader should choose three or four key passages from Jonah 4, reading them slowly, leaving plenty of space between the chosen sections.

4. After you have pictured the scenes in your mind, imagine yourself sitting alongside Jonah, waiting for the smoke to go up. What might God be saying to you through apparent inaction? And what might Christians be doing about the thousands 'who do not know their right hand from their left, and also many animals'?

5. End with silence, music or a quiet song and a final prayer.

6. There may be things members want to note down in a journal or share with others. Go on reflecting on the passage, on your meditation, and on encountering the God of Jesus Christ through the coming week.

Liturgical Resources

This section suggests ways of incorporating the study material into the Ministry of the Word as the congregation gathers on Sundays or during the week. A short series of sermons is envisaged, one for each chapter.

For each Sunday we have provided a table of readings and very brief comments, linked to material in the Church of England's *Common Worship*. There are no suggestions for music and songs because of the range of sources used by different churches.

For churches following a seasonal calendar, the material in this book is best used in Ordinary Time.

Chapter 1: A Prophet in Rebellion – Jonah 1
The Ministry of the Word

Jonah 1
Psalm 107
Acts 27.13-38
Matthew 20.17-19

The opening chapter of Jonah introduces us to a rebellious prophet and a persistent God of salvation. Psalm 107 includes a graphic description of a storm at sea and its effects on sailors (vv. 23-32). The whole psalm celebrates God's saving power. The passage from Acts is part of the account of the shipwreck that Paul had warned against in the course of his journey to Italy. The Gospel is one of Jesus' predictions of his death and resurrection after three days – often seen as foretold in Jonah.

The prayers
The meditative prayers included in this section might be adapted to be used as collects or as part of the intercessions.

Themes for the intercessions might include prayers for those suffering turbulence of any kind, those tempted to run away from the calling of God, and thanksgiving for God's deliverance.

Common Worship: Daily Prayer provides the following prayer, based on Psalm 107. This might be used at various points during the service (e.g. following a silence after the Psalm has been said or sung, or following the Address, or towards the end of the service). It is suggested that the prayer should be said by the congregation as a whole.

> O God, your steadfast love endures for ever
> and your faithfulness from one generation to another;
> rescue your people from their distress,
> still the storms of our self-will
> and bring us to the haven you have prepared for us
> in Jesus Christ our Lord.
>
> *Common Worship: Daily Prayer*: p. 742

Chapter 2: Out of the Deep – Jonah 2
The Ministry of the Word

Jonah 2
Psalm 130
Romans 11.25-36
Matthew 27.38-44

The second chapter of Jonah is a prayer poem offered by the prophet from the belly of the fish. The passage ends with the deliverance of Jonah. The psalmist cries out from the depths, urgently waiting for the mercy of God. In the passage from Romans, Paul points to God as the deliverer of those who had been disobedient to God. The Gospel reading portrays the derision of the bystanders at the crucifixion of Jesus, and their mocking call for God to deliver him.

The prayers
The meditative prayers included in this section might be adapted to be used as collects or as part of the intercessions.

Themes for the intercessions might include prayers for those who feel trapped or overwhelmed by the circumstances of their lives, those who are despairing, and those in the grip of pride and prejudice.

Give thanks that God meets us at the lowest point of our need.

Common Worship: Daily Prayer provides the following prayer, based on Psalm 130.

> Lord of mercy and redemption,
> rescue us, we pray, from the depths of sin and death;
> forgive us what we do wrong,
> and give us grace to stand in your presence,
> to serve you in Jesus Christ our Lord.
>
> *Common Worship: Daily Prayer*: p. 779

Common Worship: Daily Prayer also provides a Litany, which might be used towards the end of the intercessions. It could be used by different groups of voices, e.g. leader and congregation, each side of the church gathering alternately, or women and men.

> O Lord, answer us in the day of trouble,
> send us help from your holy place.
>
> Show us the path of life,
> for in your presence is joy.
>
> Give justice to the orphan and oppressed
> and break the power of wickedness and evil.
>
> Look upon the hungry and sorrowful
> and grant them the help for which they long.
>
> Let the heavens rejoice and the earth be glad;
> may your glory endure for ever.
>
> Your kingship has dominion over all
> and with you is our redemption.
>
> *Common Worship: Daily Prayer*: p. 348

Chapter 3: Mission Accomplished – Jonah 3
The Ministry of the Word

Jonah 3
Psalm 145
Acts 15.1-5
Matthew 18.1-5

In the passage from Jonah the prophet finally delivers God's message and the whole population of Nineveh, both human and animal, responds with repentance. The psalmist extols the grace, mercy and forgiveness of God. The passage from Acts is part of the preparation for the Council at Jerusalem, when a momentous decision was taken to honour God's inclusivity. For some Christians, conversion was not complete without adherence to Jewish law and practice. The Gospel sets out the change in behaviour and character that Jesus looked for in those who would be his disciples.

The prayers
The meditative prayers included in this section might be adapted to be used as collects or as part of the intercessions.

Themes for the intercessions might include prayers for those who need to hear and heed God's call to repentance, for those called to be God's prophets, and for a deeper sense that God's compassion is over all he has made.

Give thanks that God's love and mercy extend to all who turn to him.

The following Affirmation of Commitment from *New Patterns for Worship* might effectively be used at an appropriate point in the service, e.g. after saying the Creed or an Affirmation of Faith.

> Will you continue in the apostles' teaching
> and fellowship,
> in the breaking of bread,
> and in the prayers?

All   **With the help of God, I will.**

> Will you persevere in resisting evil and,
> whenever you fall into sin, repent and return
> to the Lord?

All   **With the help of God, I will.**

Will you proclaim by word and example
the good news of God in Christ?

All   **With the help of God, I will.**

Will you seek and serve Christ in all people,
loving your neighbour as yourself?

All   **With the help of God, I will.**

Will you acknowledge Christ's authority
    over human society,
by prayer for the world and its leaders,
by defending the weak, and by seeking peace
    and justice?

All   **With the help of God, I will.**

New Patterns for Worship: p. 169

Chapter 4: Exploring Anger – Jonah 4
The Ministry of the Word

Jonah 4
Psalm 96
Ephesians 4.25-32
Matthew 5.21-24

At the end of the Book of Jonah, we still do not know whether Jonah finally accepted God's mercy and grace for all people. We ourselves are left facing that challenge. The psalmist rejoices in God's loving sovereignty over all the earth. The passage from Ephesians forms part of the writer's recommendations for the lifestyle appropriate to those who have accepted Jesus Christ as their Lord. The Gospel is part of the Sermon on the Mount, in which Jesus explores behaviour and relationships.

The prayers

The meditative prayers included in this section might be adapted to be used as collects or as part of the intercessions.

Themes for the intercessions might include prayers for those who are angry with God, for those possessed by prejudice and self-righteousness.

Give thanks that God probes us with his searching love.

Common Worship: Daily Prayer provides the following prayer, based on Psalm 96. Just as Jonah was sent to proclaim good news of deliverance to all, so are we.

> Lord God, whom we worship in the beauty
>   of holiness,
> receive our prayer,
> as we tell out your salvation
> and declare your glory to all nations,
> that all the earth may see your righteous deeds
> and glorify your holy name;
> through Jesus Christ our Lord.

Common Worship: Daily Prayer: p. 720

Notes

CHAPTER 1

1. 'The Hound of Heaven' is a poem by Francis Thompson. See, for example, *The Oxford Book of Christian Verse*, Clarendon, 1940, p. 510.
2. From 'Morning Prayer from *The Book of Common Prayer*', *Common Worship*, Church House Publishing, 2000, p. 64.

CHAPTER 2

1. From Julian of Norwich, *Revelations of Divine Love*, Penguin Books, 1966, p. 211.
2. From *Revelations of Divine Love*, p. 70.

CHAPTER 3

1. These words are from the hymn 'Songs of praise the angels sang', which is no. 196 in *Hymns Ancient & Modern New Standard*, Hymns Ancient & Modern Limited, 1983.

CHAPTER 4

1. From *Revelations of Divine Love*, p. 68.
2. From 'The Collar', *The English Poems of George Herbert*, C. A. Patrides (ed.), Dent, 1974, p. 161.
3. From 'The Clod and the Pebble', *William Blake, A Selection of Poems and Letters*, J. Bronowski (ed.), Penguin, 1958, p. 42.

Further Reading

Most standard Bible commentaries or series of commentaries will contain sections or volumes on Jonah.

In addition, the following are very helpful:

Rosemary Nixon, *The Message of Jonah (The Bible Speaks Today Series)*, IVP, 2003.

Eugene H. Peterson, *Under the Unpredictable Plant: An Exploration of Vocational Holiness*, Eerdmans, 1994. Peterson uses the book of Jonah to explore the theme of vocation, with particular reference to pastoral ministry.

Notes on the Order for Daily Prayer

Christians in every generation have found it helpful to pray and listen to Scripture using a prepared form, sometimes called a Daily Office. A very simple office is provided here for readers who are not used to praying in this way and who want to set their Bible reading in the context of daily prayer.

It is helpful to find a regular time and place each day. Choose the time of day that is most convenient and helpful for you. There are six sections in each chapter and psalms are suggested for the six weekdays. The preparation begins with a sentence of Scripture, an opening psalm and an opportunity for quiet prayer.

The Word of God suggests a psalm for each day. The psalms chosen reflect the themes that are found in Jonah. There is then space to read the set Bible passage and notes.

The prayers are in response to the Word of God. Offer your own prayers of intercession in the place suggested. It may help to keep a short list of people and situations you pray for regularly.

Much of the material here is taken from Morning and Evening Prayer in *Common Worship*. If you find this way of praying helpful, you may want to explore a more developed form of the Daily Office. One example, with a rich variety of material, is *Common Worship: Daily Prayer Preliminary Edition*, Church House Publishing, 2002.

An Order for Daily Prayer

Preparation

Deliverance belongs to the Lord! (Jonah 2.9)

The Canticle
The Benedictus

Blessed be the Lord the God of Israel,
who has come to his people and set them free.

He has raised up for us a mighty Saviour,
born of the house of his servant David.

Through his holy prophets God promised of old
to save us from our enemies,
    from the hands of all that hate us,

To show mercy to our ancestors,
and to remember his holy covenant.

This was the oath God swore to our father Abraham:
to set us free from the hands of our enemies,

Free to worship him without fear,
holy and righteous in his sight
all the days of our life.

And you, child, shall be called the prophet of the
    Most High,
for you will go before the Lord to prepare his way,

To give his people knowledge of salvation
by the forgiveness of all their sins.

In the tender compassion of our God
the dawn from on high shall break upon us,

> To shine on those who dwell in darkness and the
>   shadow of death,
> and to guide our feet into the way of peace.
>
> Glory to the Father and to the Son
> and to the Holy Spirit;
> as it was in the beginning is now
> and shall be for ever. Amen.

Common Worship: p. 34

The Word of God

Daily psalms

Monday	55
Tuesday	139
Wednesday	69
Thursday	100
Friday	103
Saturday	148

Bible reading (using the passage for the day)

Reflection on the Bible reading

Reading the notes

Prayers

The short prayer for the day (from the notes)

Intercessions are offered

The Lord's Prayer
Our Father in heaven,
hallowed be your name,
your kingdom come,
your will be done,
on earth as in heaven.
Give us today our daily bread.
Forgive us our sins
as we forgive those who sin against us.
Lead us not into temptation
but deliver us from evil.
For the kingdom, the power,
and the glory are yours
now and for ever.
Amen.

Almighty God,
we thank you for the gift of your holy word.
May it be a lantern to our feet,
a light upon our paths,
and a strength to our lives.
Take us and use us
to love and serve all people
in the power of the Holy Spirit
and in the name of your Son,
Jesus Christ our Lord.
Amen.

Common Worship: p. 47

Emmaus Bible Resources – other titles in the series

Emmaus Bible Resources – Ideal for small groups!

Finding a middle ground between daily Bible notes and weighty commentaries, the series adopts the Emmaus approach of combining sound theology and good educational practice with a commitment to equip the whole Church for mission.

Each book contains leader's guidelines, short prayers or meditations, a commentary, discussion questions and practical 'follow-on' activities.

The Lord is Risen!: Luke 24

Steven Croft

£7.95   0 7151 4971 7

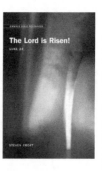

The 50 days from Easter to Pentecost are a unique period in the history of the Christian faith. *The Lord is Risen!* takes us on a journey through Luke that strengthens, challenges, deepens and renews our Christian discipleship. An ideal 'Easter' book.

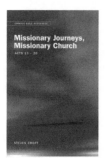

Missionary Journeys, Missionary Church: Acts 13–20

Steven Croft

£7.95   0 7151 4972 5

The book of Acts is the most exciting and dramatic in the New Testament. Throughout Christian history, men and women have returned to the book of Acts to find their faith and ministry renewed and rekindled.

Christ our Life: Colossians

David Day

£7.95   0 7151 4987 3

Colossians was written to a church set in a culture dominated by powerful forces and alternative spiritualities. The challenges to the Church in the twenty-first century are strikingly similar, making Paul's letter as relevant to Christians today, as it was to the Colossians. His key message was that Christ shall have first place in everything.

David Day's perceptive book encourages us to consider how to give Christ his rightful place in every area of our lives, both personal and corporate.

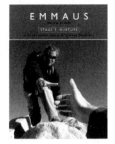

If you have enjoyed using this Emmaus Bible Resource, you may be interested in *Emmaus: The Way of Faith*. This resource is designed to help churches welcome people into the Christian faith and the life of the Church.

Emmaus has three stages – contact, nurture and growth. It encourages the vision of the local church for evangelism and gives practical advice on how to develop contact with those outside the Church. The course material provided includes a 15-week nurture course that covers the basics of the Christian life and four growth books that offer Christians an opportunity to deepen their understanding of Christian living and discipleship.

All the group notes are fully photocopiable.

The authors are Stephen Cottrell, Steven Croft, John Finney, Felicity Lawson, Robert Warren.

Visit our web site www.e-mmaus.org.uk, email any enquiries to: emmaus@c-of-e.org.uk or call 020 7898 1524.

Emmaus: The Way of Faith

Introduction: 2nd edition

£4.95   0 7151 4963 6

Essential background to both the theology and practice of Emmaus and includes material on how to run the course in your own church.

Leading an Emmaus Group

£5.95   0 7151 4905 9

Straightforward and direct guide to leading both Nurture and Growth groups. It lays a biblical framework for group leadership, using Jesus as the example and model.

Contact: 2nd Edition

£5.95   0 7151 4995 4

Explores ways that your church can be involved in evangelism and outreach and make contact with those outside the Church.

Nurture: 2nd Edition

£22.50   0 7151 4994 6

A 15-session course covering the basics of Christian life and faith.

Growth: Knowing God

£17.50   0 7151 4875 3

Four short courses for growing Christians: Living the Gospel; Knowing the Father; Knowing Jesus; and Come, Holy Spirit.

Growth: Growing as a Christian

£17.50   0 7151 4876 1

Five short courses for growing Christians: Growing in Prayer; Growing in the Scriptures; Being Church; Growing in Worship; and Life, Death and Christian Hope.

Growth: Christian Lifestyle

£15.00   0 7151 4877 X

Four short courses for growing Christians: Living Images; Overcoming Evil; Personal Identity; and Called into Life.

Growth: Your Kingdom Come

£15.00   0 7151 4904 0

This Growth book looks in depth at two main issues: the Beatitudes and the Kingdom.

Youth Emmaus

£19.95   0 7151 4988 1

Aimed specifically at young people aged 11-16 Youth Emmaus tackles the basics of the Christian faith.

Related Titles

Travelling Well: A Companion Guide to the Christian Faith

Stephen Cottrell and Steven Croft

£6.95   0 7151 4935 0

Provides instruction for important areas in Christian life such as prayer, reading the Bible, worship and relating faith to daily life. Ideal for adult Christians who are beginning the journey of faith.